THE RICHEST MAN IN BABYLON

Updated in Modern English for Today's Reader

Rendered Into Modern Language by:
Marty Hale

STRAIGHT
TRUTH PRESS

Straight Truth Press

The Richest Man in Babylon: Updated in Modern English for Today's Reader
Adapted and Modernized by Marty Hale
Based on *The Richest Man in Babylon* by George S. Clason (public domain)

Paperback ISBN: 979-8-9992267-4-7
eBook ISBN: 979-8-9992267-5-4

Cover design by the author
Printed in the United States of America

Table of Contents

Introduction

This modern edition of *The Richest Man in Babylon* brings timeless financial wisdom into the language of today. First written in 1926 by George S. Clason, the original book used stories from ancient Babylon to teach foundational truths about money, discipline, and building wealth.

But while the message has endured, the language often hasn't. That's why this edition—*The Richest Man in Babylon: Updated in Modern English for Today's Reader*—was carefully adapted and modernized by Marty Hale.

No principles have been added or removed. The aim was simple: to make this classic clearer, more accessible, and more practical for today's readers. Archaic terms have been updated. Long speeches shortened. But the truth remains the same.

These are the same time-tested principles that led ancient merchants, laborers, and leaders to prosperity:

- Spend less than you earn.
- Make your money work for you.
- Guard your wealth against loss.
- Invest in your skills.

This isn't just another financial book—it's the one that changed my life.

Reading *The Richest Man in Babylon* in my early business journey gave me a roadmap for success and financial freedom. I've since used these same principles to build companies, lead teams, and mentor others in business. If you want to learn more about my business background, contact me at marty@straighttruthpress.com.

Whether you're starting your financial journey or rebuilding after setbacks, this book offers a clear path forward—one coin at a time.

Adapted and modernized by Marty Hale
Based on the public domain work by George S. Clason
2025 — Straight Truth Press

The Man Who Desired Gold

Bansir built chariots for a living in Babylon. But today, he sat there, slouched on the short wall outside his house, feeling defeated.

He looked over at his small home and the open-air shop where a half-built chariot waited to be finished.

His wife kept peeking out the door, shooting him worried looks that meant, *"Food's running low. You should be working."*

She was right. The job still needed a lot—hammering the frame, shaping the wood, polishing and painting, tightening the leather around the wheels. Once it was done, he could deliver it and get paid by the rich man who ordered it.

But Bansir didn't move. He just sat there, stocky and strong, but stuck in his thoughts. His mind was trying to solve something he didn't understand, no matter how hard he tried.

The sun was blazing hot, just like it always was in the valley by the Euphrates River. Sweat dripped down his face and into his chest hair, but he didn't even notice.

Just beyond Bansir's home rose the massive stone walls of the king's palace, stacked high in grand terraces. Not far off, the colorful tower of the Temple of Bel reached into the bright blue sky.

His little house sat humbly in the shadow of all that wealth and power. It wasn't much, but it was tidy—better kept than many others around it. That was Babylon: rich and poor living side by side. Huge palaces and temples next to run-down shacks. Wealth and poverty jammed together with no real plan, all inside the city's protective walls.

Behind him, if he had bothered to turn around, the streets were alive with noise. Ornate chariots jostled past tradesmen in sandals and beggars with bare feet. Even the rich sometimes had to step into the gutter to make room for long lines of slaves hauling heavy bags of water. These water carriers were working for the king, pouring water into the famous hanging gardens.

But Bansir didn't notice any of it. His mind was too wrapped up in his worries.

A Musician's Arrival

Then something broke through his thoughts—the soft, familiar sound of a lyre being strummed. He looked up and saw the smiling face of his best friend, Kobbi the musician.

"May the gods bless you with great wealth, my friend!" Kobbi said with a playful grin and an exaggerated bow. "Although, from the looks of it, they already have—since you clearly don't need to work! I'm happy for your good fortune. In fact, I'd love to share in it.

How about you fish out just two little shekels from that overflowing money pouch of yours and loan them to me until after the noblemen's feast tonight? You won't even miss them before I pay you back."

"If I *had* two shekels," Bansir said with a heavy sigh, "I couldn't lend them to anyone—not even to you, my best friend—because they'd be all I have. And nobody lends out *everything* they own, not even to their best friend."

"What?" Kobbi said, genuinely shocked. "You don't even have *one* shekel in your purse, and yet here you are sitting on a wall doing nothing? Why aren't you finishing that chariot? How else are you going to feed that big appetite of yours? This isn't like you at all. What's going on? Are you in trouble? Has something happened?"

A Dream Too Good to Be True

"It must be a curse from the gods," Bansir said, shaking his head. "It started with a dream—such a strange dream. In it, I was wealthy. A heavy leather purse hung from my belt, stuffed with coins.

There were bronze shekels I tossed to beggars without a second thought, silver pieces I used to buy fine clothes for my wife and anything I wanted for myself, and even gold coins that made me feel safe about the future, so spending the silver didn't worry me at all. I felt completely content! You'd wouldn't have known me—no longer the weary craftsman you see every day. And my wife—her face was smooth and happy again, like when we first married."

"Sounds wonderful," Kobbi said. "But why would such a pleasant dream leave you sitting here like a stone?"

"Because when I woke up, my purse was still empty, and anger welled up inside me." Bansir motioned for Kobbi to sit. "Let's talk this through, because we're in the same boat. As boys we studied together, as young men we chased the same pleasures, and as adults we've stayed close friends.

We've always served our king faithfully. We've worked long hours and spent our wages freely. Over the years we've earned good money—yet to feel what real wealth is like, we have to *dream* about it. Isn't that absurd?

We live in the richest city on earth—travelers say no other place has this much gold—yet we own nothing. After a lifetime of hard work, you, my best friend, ask to borrow a mere two shekels for tonight's feast, and I have to admit my purse is as empty as yours. What's wrong with us? Why can't we hold on to silver and gold—enough for more than just food and simple clothes?

"Think of our sons," Bansir went on. "They're following the same path as we did. Will they, and their children after them, live their whole lives surrounded by treasure yet settle for sour goat's milk and porridge like we do?"

Kobbi frowned. "I've never heard you talk this way."

"I've never *thought* this way until now," Bansir answered. "From dawn until dark I build the finest chariots, hoping the gods will notice my hard work and reward me. They never have—and I finally realize they never will.

I want to own land and cattle, to wear fine robes, to hear coins jingle in my purse. I'm willing to work for it with my back, my hands, and my mind—but I want fair reward for my labor. So tell me again: why can't we claim our share of the good things that are everywhere for those who have the gold to buy them?"

"I wish I had an answer," Kobbi said. "But I'm just as frustrated as you. The money I earn from my lyre disappears fast. I'm constantly figuring out ways to make sure my family doesn't go hungry.

And deep down, I've got this longing—to own a big lyre. One that could really let me play the music I hear in my head. With that kind of instrument, I could create music more beautiful than even the king has ever heard."

"You *should* have a lyre like that," Bansir said. "No one in all Babylon could play it better. The king would be amazed. Even the gods might stop and listen. But how can you ever get one, when both of us are as broke as the king's slaves?"

Like Slaves Without Chains
He paused, then nodded toward the street. "Listen—the bell. Here they come."

A long line of half-naked, sweating men marched up the narrow street from the river, five across, each one bent over with the weight of a goatskin filled with water.

"Look at the man in front with the bell," Kobbi said. "No load, just leading the group. Looks like someone important in his homeland."

"There are a lot of strong men in that line," Bansir added. "Look—tall, light-haired men from the north… laughing black men from the south… smaller men from nearby lands. All of them walking back and forth, day after day, from the river to the hanging gardens. No joy to look forward to. They sleep on straw and eat hard porridge. I feel sorry for them, Kobbi."

"So do I," Kobbi said quietly. "But when I really think about it… are we that much better off? Sure, we call ourselves free, but how different are our lives?"

"You're right," Bansir nodded. "It's a hard truth, but it's true. We don't want to keep living like this—year after year, working and working and still getting nowhere."

"Then why don't we find out how others get gold?" Kobbi asked. "Maybe we can do what they do."

"Maybe there's a secret," Bansir said, his voice picking up hope. "Maybe someone who *knows* could teach us."

"This very day," Kobbi said, "I saw our old friend Arkad riding by in his golden chariot. And I'll tell you something— he didn't act too proud to notice me. He waved for everyone to see and gave me a big smile. That meant a lot."

"They say he's the richest man in all Babylon," Bansir said thoughtfully.

"Rich enough," Kobbi added, "that the king asks him for help with the royal treasury."

Bansir let out a laugh. "So rich, I'd be tempted to empty his bulging purse if I bumped into him in a dark alley!"

Kobbi rolled his eyes. "Come on, now. A man's wealth isn't just the money in his purse. A fat purse means nothing if it doesn't keep getting refilled. Arkad has a steady *income*—that's what keeps his money flowing no matter how much he spends."

"Income," Bansir said, repeating the word with wonder. "That's it! I want *that*. Money coming in all the time, whether I'm working or not. Arkad must know how a man can make that happen. You think someone like me could understand how he does it?"

"I think he taught his son, Nomasir," Kobbi said. "Remember? He sent him to Nineveh without a single coin from the family fortune. And from what people say at the inn, Nomasir became one of the richest men there—all on his own."

A Plan to Seek Wisdom

"Kobbi, that gives me hope," Bansir said, his eyes lighting up. "It doesn't cost anything to ask a friend for advice—and Arkad has always been a good friend. Who cares if our purses are empty? That shouldn't stop us.

We're tired of being broke while living in the richest city in the world. We *want* to be men of means. Come on—let's go talk to Arkad. Let's ask him how we can start building income for ourselves."

"You've really opened my eyes, Bansir," Kobbi said. "You've helped me understand something I never saw before. The reason we've never gained wealth… is because we never truly *sought* it.

"You've put your heart into building the strongest chariots in Babylon—and you succeeded at that. I've poured myself into playing the lyre—and I became good at it.

"In the things we gave our best effort, we succeeded. And the gods, it seems, were content to let us stay where we were. But now… finally, we see a new light—bright and clear like the rising sun.

That light is calling us to *learn*, so we can *grow*. With this new understanding, we can find honorable ways to get what we've always hoped for."

"Then let's go to Arkad today," Bansir urged. "And let's invite a few of our old friends from childhood—men who, like us, haven't fared much better. They might benefit from his wisdom too."

"You've always looked out for your friends, Bansir," Kobbi said with a smile. "That's why you have so many. Yes—let's go today. And we'll take them with us."

The Richest Man in Babylon

In ancient Babylon, there once lived a man named Arkad—well known throughout the land for being incredibly wealthy.

He was also known for being generous. He gave freely to charities. He provided well for his family. He wasn't stingy with his own comforts, either. And yet, no matter how much he spent, his wealth continued to grow—year after year, faster than he could spend it.

The Friends Come Seeking Answers

One day, some of his old friends from their younger years came to see him. They said:

"Arkad, you're clearly more fortunate than we are. You've become the richest man in all Babylon, while we're still barely scraping by. You wear the finest clothes and eat the best food, while we're just trying to make sure our families are decently dressed and have enough to eat.

"But we used to be equals. We studied under the same teacher. We played the same games. And back then, you weren't any better than us—at learning or at sports. And since then, you've been no more honorable or hardworking than we have, at least as far as we can tell.

"So why is it that fate has chosen you for such good fortune, while leaving us behind—when we're just as deserving?"

Arkad shook his head and replied:

"If you've done no better than barely survive all these years, it's either because you never learned the principles that lead to building wealth—or you learned them and chose not to follow them."

Fickle Fate and Foolish Fortune

"'Fickle Fate,'" Arkad said, "is a cruel goddess. She never brings lasting good to anyone. More often than not, she brings disaster to the very people she showers with unearned wealth.

"Some become reckless spenders—lavish with their money, throwing it around without thought. But soon, it's all gone. And worse, they're left with expensive tastes and desires they can no longer afford to satisfy.

"Others become hoarders, clinging to every coin out of fear. They're too afraid to spend even a little, because they know they didn't earn it and don't know how to replace it. These people live in constant fear of thieves, and they trap themselves in lonely, miserable lives.

"Now, there may be a few—very few—who receive sudden wealth and manage to grow it and live wisely and happily. But they are rare. I've only heard of such people secondhand.

"Think about the men you know who have inherited large sums. Haven't most of them lost it or lived unhappily?"

His friends nodded. Yes, among those they knew who had come into money, Arkad's words rang true. So they pleaded with him:

"Then tell us how *you* became so wealthy."

So Arkad continued:

"When I was young, I looked around and saw all the good things life had to offer—comfort, beauty, satisfaction. And I realized something: **wealth makes all of those things more possible**. Wealth is power.

"With it, you can furnish your home with the finest things. You can sail to far-off lands. You can enjoy foods from distant countries. You can buy beautiful jewelry crafted by skilled goldsmiths and stonecutters. You can even build great temples to honor the gods."

"With wealth," Arkad said, "you can enjoy all these things—and many others that bring pleasure to the senses and fulfillment to the soul.

"When I realized this, I made a decision: I would not stand off to the side, watching others enjoy the good things in life while I went without. I wouldn't settle for dressing in cheap clothes that were just barely respectable. I wouldn't accept a poor man's life as my fate.

"No, I decided I would claim my seat at the banquet of life's blessings.

"As you know, I was the son of a simple merchant, one of many children, with no chance of inheritance. And as you've kindly pointed out, I didn't have any special talent or wisdom beyond the rest of you. So I came to one clear conclusion: if I wanted to live a better life, it would take time and study.

"Time, I had. We all have it. And truthfully, each of you has let enough time slip by that you could have built wealth by now—if only you had known how. As it stands, you have little to show for it, other than your good families, which you can rightly be proud of.

"As for study," he went on, "didn't our teacher tell us that learning comes in two forms? One is what we already know. The other is how to find out what we don't know.

"So I made up my mind: I would learn how to build wealth—and once I discovered the way, I would commit myself to it fully. Isn't it wise to enjoy the sunlight while we can? There will be time enough for sorrow when we pass into the darkness of the spirit world.

"I got a job as a scribe in the Hall of Records. Day after day, I worked long hours writing on clay tablets. Week after week, month after month, I toiled—and yet, I had nothing to show for it. My earnings disappeared into food, clothes, offerings to the gods, and other expenses I can't even remember.

"But I didn't give up. I stayed determined."

The Scribe and the Moneylender

One day, a man named Algamish—the well-known money lender—came into the Hall of Records and placed an order for a copy of the Ninth Law. He looked directly at me and said, "I need this finished in two days. If you get it done by then, I'll pay you two copper coins."

So I worked hard. But the law was long and detailed, and when Algamish returned, I hadn't finished. He was furious. If I had been his slave, I'm sure he would've beaten me on the spot.

But I wasn't afraid—because I knew the city master wouldn't allow him to harm me. So I spoke up. I said, "Algamish, you're a wealthy man. Tell me how I can become wealthy too, and I'll stay up all night carving the rest. By sunrise, it'll be done."

He looked at me, amused, and said, "You're a bold one. But all right—we'll call it a deal."

That night, I worked without stopping. My back ached, and the smell of the oil lamp made my head pound. My eyes were so tired I could barely see. But by the time the sun came up, the tablets were finished.

When he returned in the morning, I said, "I've done my part. Now tell me what you promised."

"You've kept your word, my son," he said warmly, "and I will keep mine. I'll tell you what you want to know—because I'm getting old, and old men like to talk. When young people ask for advice, they're getting the benefit of many years of experience.

"But too often," he added, "youth thinks that old men only know things from the past—and so they ignore that wisdom. That's a mistake.

"Remember this: the same sun that shines today shone when your father was born, and it will still be shining when your last grandchild leaves this world.

"Youthful thinking," he said, "is like a shooting star—bright and exciting but short-lived. The wisdom of age is like the fixed stars in the night sky—steady and dependable. Sailors use them to steer their ships. You can build your life on wisdom like that."

"Listen closely to what I'm about to say," Algamish told me. "If you don't, you'll miss the truth I'm trying to give you—and then all your hard work last night will have been for nothing."

The First Law of Wealth
He looked at me sharply from under his thick eyebrows. Then, in a firm and quiet voice, he said, "I found the path to wealth the day I decided that a *part of everything I earned was mine to keep*. And that's how *you* will find it too."

He stared at me intently, saying nothing more. I could feel his eyes boring into me.

"That's it?" I asked.

"That truth alone was enough to turn a poor shepherd into a wealthy moneylender," he said.

"But... all I earn is mine to keep, isn't it?" I asked, confused.

"Far from it," he replied. "Don't you pay the clothes maker? The sandal maker? Don't you pay for food, for shelter? Can anyone live in Babylon without spending money?

"Think about it—what do you have left to show for everything you earned last month? What about the past year?

"You fool," he said bluntly. "You pay everyone… but *yourself.* You work hard, but your money goes to others. You might as well be a slave—working to earn food and clothes handed to you by your master.

"But imagine this," he continued. "If you had saved just *one-tenth* of everything you earned, how much would you have in ten years?"

My training in numbers didn't fail me. I answered, "As much as I earn in a whole year."

"You're only half right," he said. "Every gold coin you save becomes a little worker for you. And every coin *it* earns becomes another little worker. If you truly want to become wealthy, your savings must earn for you—and their earnings must earn too. That's how you build real abundance.

"You may think I cheated you by giving you just one idea for your long night's work," he said. "But I'm actually paying you a *thousand times over*—if you're smart enough to understand the value of the truth I just gave you."

"Remember," Algamish said, "*a part of everything you earn is yours to keep.* Make it no less than one-tenth—no matter how small your wages—though you can certainly save more if you're able. **Pay yourself first.** After that, buy only what you can afford: clothes, sandals, food, offerings to the gods, and charity—all from the remaining nine-tenths.

"Wealth is like a tree that grows from a single seed. The first copper you save is that seed. Plant it soon, and your tree starts growing sooner. Water it faithfully—keep saving—and before long you'll rest in the shade of its abundance."

With that, he picked up his tablets and left.

I thought long and hard about his words, and they made sense. So I tested his advice. Every time I got paid, I took one coin out of every ten and hid it away. Oddly enough, I never felt short of money; I managed just fine without that tenth. As my stash grew, I was tempted to spend it on the tempting goods traders brought from Phoenicia—but I resisted.

A year later, Algamish returned and asked, "My son, have you paid yourself at least one-tenth of all you earned this past year?"

Proudly I answered, "Yes, Master, I have."

"Excellent," he said, smiling. "And what have you done with it?"

Hard Lessons, Wise Investment

"I gave it to Azmur the brick-maker," I said. "He's sailing to Tyre to buy rare Phoenician jewels. When he gets back, we'll sell them at a high price and split the profit."

Algamish scowled. "Every fool must learn. Tell me—since when does a brick-maker know anything about jewels? Would you ask a baker about the stars? Of course not—you'd go to an astrologer, if you were thinking clearly.

"Your savings are gone, boy—you've yanked your wealth-tree out by the roots. Plant another and try again. Next time, if you want advice about jewels, talk to a jewel merchant. Seek sheep advice from a herdsman. **Advice is free, but only take what's worth having.** If you trust your savings to someone who knows nothing about money, you'll pay for their ignorance with your own coins."

With that, he turned and left.

And just as Algamish had warned, it turned out he was right. The Phoenicians were swindlers. They sold Azmur worthless pieces of colored glass that only *looked* like jewels. My savings were gone.

But I remembered what Algamish had said. So I started over and continued to save one-tenth of everything I earned. By now it had become a habit, and honestly, it wasn't even hard anymore.

Twelve months later, Algamish came back to the scribe room and asked, "What progress have you made since I last saw you?"

"I've kept paying myself faithfully," I told him. "This time I gave my savings to Agger the shieldmaker. He uses it to buy bronze, and every fourth month, he pays me a share of the profits—like rent."

"That's good," he said. "And what do you do with the money he pays you?"

"Well," I said proudly, "I've had some fine feasts—with honey, good wine, and spiced cakes. I bought myself a bright red tunic. And one day soon, I'll buy a young donkey to ride."

At that, Algamish burst out laughing. "You're eating the children of your savings! How do you expect them to work for you if you spend them? And how can they have *their* children—who could also work for you? First build yourself an army of little golden slaves. *Then* you can enjoy all the feasts and wine you want—without regret."

Then, once again, he went on his way.

I didn't see him again for two years. When he finally returned, he looked older—his face lined, his eyes tired and heavy. He came to me and asked, "Arkad, have you reached the wealth you once dreamed of?"

"Not everything I hope for yet," I answered, "but I have a good amount now. And it earns more—and *that* income also earns more."

He grinned. "And tell me—do you still take advice from brickmakers?"

"Only when it's about bricks," I replied with a smirk.

"Arkad," Algamish said, "you've learned your lessons well.

"First, you learned to live on less than you earn. Second, you learned to seek advice only from those who actually know what they're talking about—because they've lived it. And third, you've learned how to put your money to work for you.

"You've taught yourself how to earn money, how to keep it, and how to grow it. That makes you capable of handling real responsibility.

"I'm getting old. My sons only know how to *spend*—they give no thought to how wealth is *earned.* My business interests are large and more than I can manage on my own. If you're willing to go to Nippur and oversee my lands there, I will make you my partner. You will share in all that I own."

So I went to Nippur and took charge of his land, which turned out to be vast. Because I was ambitious—and because I had learned the three great principles of building wealth—I was able to increase the value of his estate by a great amount.

I became very successful. And when Algamish passed from this life into the next, I did indeed receive my share of his fortune, just as he had arranged under the law.

When Arkad finished telling his story, one of his old friends said, "You were lucky that Algamish made you his heir."

"Lucky?" Arkad replied. "Only in this: that I had the desire to prosper *before* I ever met him.

"For four years I had already proven my commitment—by saving at least one-tenth of everything I earned. Would you call a fisherman lucky if he'd spent years studying how fish behave, and could cast his nets with skill every time the wind changed?

"No. *Opportunity is a proud and stubborn goddess. She doesn't waste her time on those who are unprepared.*"

"You must have had strong willpower to keep going after losing all your first year's savings," said another. "Most people wouldn't have kept trying. That's unusual."

Will, Wealth, and the Way Forward

"Will-power?" Arkad laughed. "That's not some mystical strength that lets a man lift a load even a camel couldn't carry. Will-power is simply the unshakable intent to finish any task you set yourself.

"If I give myself a job—no matter how small—I complete it. That is how I build confidence for bigger tasks. Suppose I tell myself, 'For one hundred days, every time I cross the bridge into the city, I will pick up a pebble and toss it into the river.' On the seventh day, if I forget, I don't say, 'Tomorrow I'll throw two pebbles and call it even.' I would turn around, go back, pick up the pebble, and toss it.

"On the twentieth day I wouldn't tell myself, 'Arkad, this is pointless—just throw in a handful and be done.' I'd keep to the plan. Because when I start something, I finish it. That's also why I don't start foolish or impossible tasks—leisure is too precious to waste."

Another friend objected: "If what you say is true, and so simple, wouldn't everyone doing it use up all the wealth there is?"

"Not at all," Arkad replied. "Wealth expands wherever people apply effort. If a rich man builds a new palace, does the gold he pays disappear? No. The brick-maker gets some, the laborers get some, the artists get some—everyone who works on the palace shares in it. And when the palace is finished, the land it sits on is worth more, and even the neighboring land rises in value. Wealth grows in ways that seem almost magical. Look at the Phoenicians: they built great cities on barren coasts with the wealth their trading ships brought home."

"Then what should we do," asked another friend, "so we, too, can become rich? We're not young anymore, and we've saved nothing."

"Take Algamish's advice," Arkad said. "Repeat to yourselves: **'A part of all I earn is mine to keep.'** Say it when you wake up, at noon, at night—every hour if you must—until the words burn across your mind like letters of fire.

"Make the idea part of you. Then choose the portion—never less than one-tenth—and set it aside *first*. Adjust the rest of your spending to make that possible. Soon you'll feel the thrill of owning a treasure that belongs only to you. As it grows, it will motivate you. You'll find fresh energy to earn more—and of every extra coin you make, the same fraction will also be yours to keep."

"Next," Arkad said, "learn to make your treasure *work* for you. Turn your money into your slave—let its children and its grandchildren work for you as well.

"Secure an income for the future. Think of the elderly, and remember you will one day join their ranks. Invest your savings wisely so you don't lose them. Offers of impossibly high returns are like sirens: they lure the careless onto the rocks of loss and regret.

"Make sure, too, that your family is provided for if the gods call you away. You can arrange such protection with small, regular payments—so don't wait for some large windfall to act.

"Seek counsel from the wise. Talk to people whose daily business is handling money. Let their experience keep you from mistakes—like the one I made when I trusted Azmur the brick-maker with my funds. A modest, reliable return is far better than a risky one.

"Finally, enjoy life while you live it. Don't over-strain or try to save every coin. If one-tenth is the most you can comfortably keep, be satisfied with that. Spend the rest within your means. Don't become so stingy that you're afraid to enjoy the good things this world offers."

Arkad's friends thanked him and departed. *Some were silent— unable to picture a new way of life. Some were cynical—thinking a rich man should simply share his fortune. But a few walked away with a new light in their eyes.*

They understood why Algamish had returned again and again to watch a scribe climb from darkness into light—because only when that man grasped the truth for himself was he ready for opportunity.

Those few came back to Arkad often in the years that followed. He welcomed them, shared his knowledge, and helped them place their savings in safe investments that earned steady returns—money that would not be lost or trapped in ventures that paid nothing.

The turning point in their lives came the day they embraced the lesson passed from Algamish to Arkad, and from Arkad to them:

A PART OF ALL YOU EARN IS YOURS TO KEEP.

Seven Cures For a Lean Purse

The glory of Babylon still echoes through history. For centuries, it has been remembered as the richest city of the ancient world—its treasures legendary, its splendor unmatched.

But Babylon wasn't always wealthy. Its riches came as a result of the **wisdom of its people**. They had to learn *how* to build wealth before they could enjoy it.

When the good King Sargon returned to Babylon after defeating the Elamites, he was met with a troubling situation. The Royal Chancellor explained it this way:

"Your Majesty, after many years of great prosperity—thanks to your leadership in building the mighty irrigation canals and the grand temples to the gods—our people now find themselves struggling.

"The construction projects are finished. The laborers are unemployed. Merchants have few customers. Farmers can't sell their crops. The people simply don't have enough gold to buy what they need."

The King frowned. "But what happened to all the gold we spent on those massive improvements?"

The Chancellor replied, "I fear, my King, that most of it has ended up in the hands of just a few wealthy men in the city. For the majority of our people, the gold passed through their hands as quickly as goat's milk through a sieve. And now that the flow of gold has stopped, they have nothing to show for all their earnings."

The King sat in silence, deep in thought. Finally, he asked, "Why is it that so few have managed to hold on to all the gold?"

"Because they *know how*," the Chancellor replied. "You can't fault a man for succeeding simply because he understands what others don't. And it wouldn't be right to take from those who've earned wealth fairly and give it to others who lack the skill."

"Then why," asked the King, "shouldn't all the people learn how to build wealth—so they, too, can become rich and prosperous?"

"That's entirely possible, Your Majesty. But who would teach them? Certainly not the priests—they know nothing of making money."

"Then who *does* know?" the King asked. "Who in Babylon understands best how to grow wealth?"

"Your question answers itself, sire," the Chancellor replied. "Who is the richest man in Babylon?"

"Well said," the King nodded. "It is Arkad. Bring him to me tomorrow."

As the King commanded, Arkad appeared the next day. Despite being seventy years old, he stood upright and full of energy.

"Arkad," said the King, "is it true that you are the richest man in Babylon?"

"So it is said, Your Majesty—and no one disputes it."

"How did you become so wealthy?"

"By taking advantage of the same opportunities available to all citizens of Babylon," Arkad replied.

"You started with nothing?"

"Nothing but a strong desire to become wealthy."

"Arkad," the King said, "our city is struggling. A few men know how to acquire wealth—and they've gathered most of the gold. But the majority of our citizens don't know how to keep the money they earn.

"I want Babylon to be the wealthiest city in the world. That means we need *many* wealthy citizens—not just a few. So we must teach everyone how to acquire riches. Tell me, Arkad— is there a secret to building wealth? Can it be taught?"

"It can, Your Majesty," Arkad replied. "What one man learns, he can teach to others."

The King's eyes lit up. "Arkad, those are the very words I hoped to hear. Will you help me in this great cause? Will you train a group of teachers—each of whom will then teach others—until we have enough instructors to spread this knowledge across the entire kingdom?"

Arkad bowed. "I am your humble servant, my King. Whatever knowledge I have, I'll gladly share—for the good of our people and the glory of Babylon. Let your Chancellor gather one hundred men, and I will teach them the **seven cures** that once fattened my own purse—when it was leaner than any in all of Babylon."

Two weeks later, in obedience to the King's command, one hundred selected men gathered in the great hall of the Temple of Learning. They sat on colorful rugs arranged in a semicircle. In the center, Arkad sat beside a small wooden table, where a sacred lamp burned slowly, releasing a rich, pleasant fragrance into the air.

"Look," whispered one student, nudging the man beside him, "there's the richest man in Babylon."

"And yet," the other replied, "he's just a man like the rest of us."

Arkad stood and addressed the gathering.

"As a loyal subject of our great King," he began, "I am here today to serve him—and to serve you. I was once a poor young man, full of desire for gold. But in time, I discovered knowledge that helped me gain it. The King has asked me to share that knowledge with you.

"I started with nothing. My beginning was humble. I had no special advantages—nothing that each one of you does not already have.

"The first place I stored my fortune was in a leather purse. And I hated how empty it was. I dreamed of it being full—heavy with coins that clinked together. That desire pushed me to search for cures to a lean purse. I found seven.

"To you who are gathered here, I will now explain those seven cures—remedies I recommend to every man who desires to gain wealth. Each day, for seven days, I will teach you one of the seven.

"Listen closely to what I share. Talk about it with me. Discuss it among yourselves. Learn these lessons well—so that you, too, may plant the seed of wealth in your own purses.

"Each of you must first learn how to build your own fortune. Only then will you be ready to teach others what you've learned.

"I will show you in simple, practical ways how to fatten your purses. This is the first step on the path to true wealth. And no man can climb higher until he has firmly planted his feet on this first step.

"So now, let us begin.

We shall consider the **First Cure**."

The First Cure: Start Your Purse to Fattening

Arkad turned to a thoughtful-looking man in the second row. "My friend," he asked, "what kind of work do you do?"

"I'm a scribe," the man replied. "I carve records onto clay tablets."

"Ah, I earned my very first copper coins doing the same work," Arkad said. "So you have the same opportunity I had to build a fortune."

Then he looked toward a red-faced man sitting farther back. "And you, tell us—what do you do to earn your bread?"

"I'm a butcher," the man answered. "I buy goats from the farmers, slaughter them, sell the meat to housewives, and the hides to sandal-makers."

"Then you, too, work and earn. And like me, you have every advantage needed to succeed."

Arkad went on, asking each man about his trade—how he earned his living. When he had spoken to them all, he addressed the group:

"Now, my students, you can see that there are many ways to earn money. Every trade is like a stream of gold—and each man, through his work, diverts a small part of that stream into his own purse. So, whether large or small, each of you has a flow of income. Would you agree?"

They all nodded—it was true.

"Then," Arkad continued, "if each of you wants to build a fortune, doesn't it make sense to begin with the income you already have?"

Again, they agreed.

Then Arkad turned to a modest-looking man who had said he was an egg merchant. "Let me ask you something," Arkad said. "If you set aside ten eggs in a basket every morning, and take out only nine each evening, what will eventually happen?"

"The basket will overflow," the man replied.

"And why is that?"

"Because each day, I put in one more egg than I take out."

Arkad turned back to the class with a smile. "Tell me—does anyone here have a lean purse?"

At first the men looked amused. Then they began to laugh. Some jokingly held up their nearly empty purses.

"Very well," Arkad said, still smiling. "Let me tell you the **first remedy** I discovered for curing a lean purse. Do exactly as I suggested to the egg merchant. For every ten coins you earn, **spend only nine**. Leave the tenth in your purse.

"Your purse will begin to grow immediately. And as its weight increases, you'll feel proud. It will give your hand satisfaction—and your soul confidence.

"Don't scoff at the simplicity of this idea. Truth is always simple. I promised to tell you how I built my fortune—and this is how it began.

"I once cursed my empty purse just like you do. But when I began keeping just one coin out of every ten, it began to fatten. And so will yours.

"Now I'll tell you something odd, though I don't fully understand why it works. Once I stopped spending more than nine-tenths of what I earned, I got along just fine. I didn't feel poorer. In fact, money started to come to me more easily than before.

"It seems a law of the gods that the man who saves a portion of what he earns attracts gold more easily… and the man whose purse is always empty—gold avoids.

"So I ask you: what do you really want?

—Is it the satisfaction of daily desires? A trinket, new clothes, more food—things quickly used up and forgotten? —Or is it real, lasting wealth—gold, land, livestock, goods, income-producing investments?

The coins you spend will buy the first. The coins you save will buy the second.

This, my students, is the **first cure** I discovered for a lean purse:

'Of every ten coins I earn, I spend but nine.'

Talk about this among yourselves. And if any man can prove this untrue, come tell me tomorrow when we meet again."

The Second Cure: Control Your Expenditures
On the second day, Arkad addressed the class:

"Some of you asked me, 'How can a man keep one-tenth of what he earns when everything he earns is already needed for expenses?' Let's tackle that question.

"Yesterday I asked: *Who among you carried a lean purse?* Every hand went up. Yet you don't all earn the same. Some of you make far more than others. Some have larger families to support. Still—every purse was equally thin.

"Here is a curious truth about human beings: **What we call 'necessary expenses' will always expand to match our income—unless we firmly say otherwise.**

"Don't confuse *needs* with *desires.* Each of us, and our families, have more wishes than our earnings can satisfy. So we spend up to the limit of our income on those desires—yet many wishes still go unfulfilled.

"Even with my wealth, do you think I can gratify every desire? Hardly. My time, strength, and appetite all have limits. Desire is endless. Like weeds in a field, new wishes pop up wherever there's room to satisfy them.

"Study your own habits carefully. You'll usually find regular expenses you can wisely reduce or eliminate. **Demand full value for every coin you spend.**

1. **Write down** everything you wish to spend money on.
2. **Identify** what is truly necessary, and what is feasible within nine-tenths of your income.

3. **Cross out** the rest—accept that those desires must wait, and don't regret it.

"Next, create a budget for those necessary expenses. **Touch not the one-tenth that fattens your purse.** Let that be your top priority. Keep refining your budget; make it your chief ally in protecting your growing savings."

A man in a rich red-and-gold robe stood up. "I'm a free man," he said. "I want to enjoy life's good things. A budget feels like slavery—telling me what I can spend and on what. That would drain the pleasure from living, turning me into a pack animal."

Arkad replied, "Who would make your budget?"

"I would," the man answered.

"Then consider a pack animal," Arkad said. "If a donkey made his own travel plan, would he load himself with jewels, rugs, and bars of gold? Of course not. He would pack hay, grain, and water—what truly serves his journey.

"A budget isn't a chain; it's a **tool**. It helps your purse grow. It lets you afford necessities *and*, as far as possible, other desires. It safeguards your most important goals from impulsive whims. Like a lamp in a dark cave, a budget reveals the leaks in your purse so you can plug them and spend purposefully.

"So here is the **Second Cure** for a lean purse:

'Budget your expenses so you have coins for necessities, pleasures, and worthwhile desire—yet never spend more than nine-tenths of your income.'

Master this, and your purse will keep growing."

The Third Cure: Make Your Gold Multiply

"Look," Arkad began on the third day, "your lean purse is beginning to fatten. You've trained yourself to keep one-tenth of everything you earn. You've learned to control your spending so your savings can grow.

"Now it's time to put that treasure to work—to make it grow even more.

"Gold sitting idle in a purse may satisfy a miser, but it earns nothing. Saving money is just the beginning. The real fortune is built from what your savings *earn* over time."

So spoke Arkad to his class.

"How then can we make our gold work for us?" he continued. "My *first* investment, I'll admit, was a failure—I lost it all. I'll tell that story later. But my *first profitable* investment was a loan I made to a man named Aggar, a shield-maker.

"Each year Aggar needed to buy large shipments of bronze brought in from across the sea. But he didn't have enough money to pay the merchants upfront. So he borrowed from people like me who had extra coins. Aggar was an honest man. He always repaid his debts—*plus* a generous interest—once he sold his shields.

"And every time he paid me interest, I reinvested it back into another loan. That way, both my capital and its earnings began to grow. It was a good feeling—watching those payments come back and make my purse heavier and heavier.

"Let me tell you something, students: **A man's wealth is not the coins in his purse. It's the steady income he builds— the golden stream that flows into his hands whether he works or rests.** That's what *everyone* wants. And that's what *you* should aim for: money that keeps coming, even while you sleep.

"I built that kind of income. So much, in fact, that people now call me the richest man in Babylon. It all started with those first loans to Aggar. From there, as my capital grew, I made more loans and more investments. First from a few sources— then from many—streams of income began pouring into my purse, ready for wise use.

"From small beginnings, I created a whole family of golden workers—each coin earning more coins. Their 'children' earned as well, and their grandchildren too. Over time, the combined efforts of all those coins built a great income.

"Let me give you an example:

A farmer, when his first son was born, set aside ten silver coins and gave them to a moneylender. He asked that they be invested until the boy turned twenty. The moneylender agreed and promised to pay a return of one-fourth the amount every four years—and to add that return back into the investment.

When the son turned twenty, the farmer returned to check on the silver. Because the interest had been compounding, the original ten coins had grown to thirty and a half.

The farmer was pleased. And since the son didn't need the money yet, he left it invested.

When the son turned fifty—long after the father had passed on—the moneylender paid him a final sum of **one hundred sixty-seven** silver coins.

So in fifty years, that small investment had grown by nearly seventeen times—all through the power of **compound interest**.

"This, then," Arkad concluded, "is the **Third Cure** for a lean purse:

Put every coin you save to work. Let it reproduce itself—just as flocks of sheep and goats grow in number—and create a steady stream of income flowing into your life.

Make your gold your servant, and it will multiply in your service."

The Fourth Cure: Guard Your Treasure from Loss

"Bad luck," Arkad told his class on the fourth day, "loves a shining target. If you don't protect the gold in your purse, it will disappear. That's why it's wise to first secure small amounts—and learn how to protect them—before the gods trust you with more."

He paused and looked at them carefully.

"Anyone who owns gold is quickly tempted by opportunities that sound promising. Often it seems like you can make huge profits if you just invest in this or that exciting venture. Friends and relatives might already be jumping in—and urging you to do the same.

"But here's the truth: the *first rule* of investing is this—**your original money must be safe**.

"What good are big profits if the money you started with is lost? I say it's not worth it. Risk always carries a cost, and too often, that cost is everything. Before you invest a single coin, examine carefully whether your money can be safely recovered. Don't let your daydreams about fast riches trick you into ignoring the danger.

"Before you loan money to anyone, ask yourself—can he really pay it back? Has he shown himself to be honest and dependable? If not, you might just be handing him a gift instead of a loan.

"And before you invest in any business, take time to learn the dangers involved. Don't put your treasure into something you don't understand."

Arkad paused again and then shared a personal story.

"My first investment was a disaster. I had saved for a full year, and I gave that money to a brickmaker named Azmur. He was headed across the sea to Tyre, and we agreed he would buy rare Phoenician jewels. When he returned, we'd sell them and split the profits.

"But the Phoenicians swindled him. They sold him worthless bits of glass. I lost everything.

"Now, with what I know, I'd instantly see the mistake. Why would I trust a brickmaker to buy jewels? He knew nothing about them.

"That mistake taught me something I never forgot: **Don't be too confident in your own judgment—especially with money.** It's far better to get advice from people who deal with money for a living. That kind of wisdom is easy to find, and it's often worth more than the gold you were planning to invest.

"In fact," he said, "if a bit of advice saves you from a bad investment, its value is equal to the money you didn't lose."

He looked around the room once more, his voice strong and clear.

"This, then, is the **fourth cure** for a lean purse—and it's one of the most important. Once your purse is full, **protect it**. Invest only where your money is safe, where you can get it back if needed, and where it will earn you a steady, fair return. And above all, seek advice from wise and experienced men who know how to handle gold."

The Fifth Cure: Make of Thy Dwelling a Profitable Investment

"If a man sets aside nine parts of his earnings to live and enjoy life," said Arkad to his class on the fifth day, "and if any portion of that nine parts can be turned into a profitable investment without harming his well-being, then all the faster will his treasure grow."

He stood before them thoughtfully, then continued.

"Far too many men in Babylon raise their families in crowded, unworthy dwellings. They pay excessive rent to demanding landlords for small, cramped quarters. Their wives have no soil in which to grow the flowers that gladden a woman's heart, and their children are left to play in filthy alleys with no space of their own."

Arkad's voice became more passionate.

"No family can fully enjoy life without a place to call their own—a small piece of land where children may dig in clean earth and a wife may tend both blossoms and herbs to nourish her household.

"To eat figs from one's own tree, to gather grapes from one's own vine—this brings joy to a man's heart. To own the roof over your head, to have a home that is yours to care for and protect, builds pride, confidence, and gives strength to your labor."

He let that sink in, then said plainly, "I tell you, every man should own the home that shelters him and his family."

"Is that beyond reach?" he asked. "No. Our great king has expanded the walls of Babylon so far that there is plenty of unused land within them—land that may be bought at a reasonable price. And the moneylenders are eager to help men buy homes. If you can provide even a portion of the cost yourself, they will gladly lend the rest—for what purpose could be more noble?

"Once your home is built, you can repay the moneylender the same way you would pay rent. But unlike rent, each payment you make reduces your debt. And in just a few years, the house becomes yours completely. You will pay only the king's taxes—and gain a valuable property for your family.

"Your heart will rejoice in ownership. Your wife will walk proudly to the river to wash your robes and return with water to nourish her garden. Your children will grow strong, playing on soil that belongs to them."

He paused, letting the image settle into their minds.

"Blessings come to the man who owns his home. It gives him security, pride, and lowers the cost of living—freeing more of his earnings for joy, for investment, and for the fulfillment of his dreams."

Then Arkad lifted his hand and gave them the fifth cure plainly:

"Own thy own home."

The Sixth Cure: Prepare Now for Your Future
"Every person's life follows the same path," Arkad told his students. "We begin in youth and age with time. No one escapes that path—unless the gods call us early. So it's only wise to prepare now for a future when we're no longer young and strong. And it's wise to plan for the day when we might no longer be here to support our families."

He looked around the room.

"If you're learning how to build wealth and beginning to save, you should also think ahead. Plan now for investments that are safe, long-lasting, and available when you need them in later years."

"There are many ways to prepare," he explained. "Some people hide money. But no matter how well it's hidden, it could still be stolen. I don't recommend that."

"Others buy land or property. If chosen wisely, real estate holds value and can produce income or be sold to support you later."

"Still others set aside a small amount of money regularly and let it grow. I know a sandal maker named Ansan. For eight years, he deposited just two silver coins each week with a money lender. He recently received a report showing his small weekly deposits had grown into more than a thousand silver pieces, thanks to the interest he earned."

"I ran the numbers for him and showed that if he keeps up those deposits for another twelve years, he'll have more than four thousand silver coins. That's enough to live on comfortably for the rest of his life."

Arkad smiled. "When such a small, consistent investment can lead to such big results, no man should ignore the importance of preparing for his old age—or for his family's protection if something happens to him."

He paused thoughtfully. "Someday, I believe wise people will create a system where many contribute small amounts, and if one dies, the group's combined fund supports his family. I think that would be a wonderful idea. But for now, it doesn't exist."

"So we must use the tools we have today. Save. Invest. Make your plans now—because a man who grows old with no savings, or a family left without support, faces a tragic end."

Arkad looked around the hall, his tone serious now.

"This is the sixth cure for a lean purse: Prepare today for the needs of tomorrow—for your old age, and for the protection of your family."

The Seventh Cure: Increase Your Ability to Earn

On the seventh day Arkad said, "Today we come to one of the most important cures for a thin purse. I'm not going to talk about gold—I'm going to talk about you: the people beneath these colorful robes. Your own habits and mind-set can work for you or against you."

He told them of a young man who had recently asked for a loan. When Arkad asked why he needed it, the fellow complained that his pay wouldn't cover his expenses. Arkad replied, "In that case you're a poor prospect for any lender, because you have no surplus with which to repay the loan. What you really need is to **earn more**. So, what are you doing to increase your earnings?"

The young man answered, "I've already asked my boss for a raise six times in two months—what more can I do?"

Arkad smiled. "We may laugh at his approach, but he did have one thing right: he **wanted** to earn more. That's the starting point. Strong, specific desire always comes before achievement. Wanting to 'be rich' is vague. Wanting to earn five extra pieces of gold is clear—something you can pursue and win. Once you've proved you can secure five, you can aim for ten, then twenty, then a hundred, and so on. Wealth grows that way, from small goals upward."

He paused. "A man's desires must be simple and definite. Too many scattered wishes pull him in every direction and defeat their own purpose."

Arkad then spoke of his early days as a modest scribe. He noticed that some scribes earned more than he did because they produced more work. So he resolved to be outdone by no one. He poured extra interest, focus, and perseverance into each tablet he carved. Before long, he was turning out more work than any of his peers—and he didn't need to ask for a raise six times before his master noticed.

"The more skill you gain, the more you can earn," Arkad said. "The craftsman who studies better tools and techniques, the lawyer or healer who trades knowledge with other experts, the merchant who finds higher-quality goods at lower prices—all raise their own value. The world moves forward because alert people keep sharpening their skills. If you stand still, you'll be left behind."

He added that a self-respecting man also:

- pays his debts promptly and avoids buying what he can't pay for,

- provides well for his family, so they speak proudly of him,
- prepares a will, so his property is divided honorably if the gods call him early,
- shows kindness to the unfortunate and thoughtfulness to loved ones.

"Cultivate your abilities," Arkad concluded. "Study, practice, act in ways that make you respect yourself. Confidence flows from competence, and with confidence you can reach the goals you set.

"These are the seven cures for an empty purse—drawn from a long life of experience. Babylon holds more gold than you imagine; there is abundance for everyone. Go and practice these truths so you may prosper. Then teach them, so every honorable citizen may share in the wealth of our great city."

Meet the Goddess of Good Luck

"If a man be lucky, there is no foretelling the
extent of his fortune.
Throw him into the Euphrates, and chances are,
he'll swim out with a pearl in his hand."

— Babylonian Proverb

The desire to be lucky lives in all of us. It was just as strong in the hearts of people four thousand years ago in Babylon as it is today. We all want to be favored by the mysterious Goddess of Good Luck.

But is there any way to actually meet her—to win her attention and receive her blessings? Is there a way to attract good fortune, rather than waiting for it?

That's the very question the men of ancient Babylon set out to answer. They were clever, curious thinkers—people who weren't satisfied to just hope. And that kind of thinking is exactly why Babylon became the wealthiest and most powerful city of its time.

Back then, there were no formal schools or colleges. But Babylon had something even more practical: a central place of learning, open to all. Among the city's towering buildings—alongside the King's palace, the Hanging Gardens, and the mighty temples—there stood another important place, though you won't find much mention of it in history books.

It was the **Temple of Learning**, where the wisdom of past generations was shared freely. Volunteer teachers led discussions on topics people cared about most. Inside those walls, all men were equals. A humble laborer could challenge the ideas of a nobleman without fear. Even a slave could debate with a prince and be heard with respect.

Among those who regularly visited the Temple of Learning was a wealthy and respected man named **Arkad**—known far and wide as **the richest man in Babylon**. He had his own meeting hall there, and nearly every evening, a large group gathered to listen, learn, and debate. The crowd was mixed—some old, some young, but mostly men in the middle of life—seeking wisdom and practical advice.

An Urgent Lesson in the Public Square
Let's sit in on one of those gatherings and see if these men knew how to attract good luck.

That evening, the sun had just slipped beneath the horizon, casting a red glow across the dusty desert sky, when Arkad strolled to his usual place at the front of the room. About eighty men were already reclining on small rugs spread across the stone floor. More were still arriving.

Arkad smiled and called out, "What shall we discuss tonight?"

After a short pause, a tall man stood up. He was a cloth weaver by trade, and as was the custom, he stood to speak respectfully.

"I have a topic in mind," he said, "but I hesitate to mention it. I fear it may sound foolish to you, Arkad, or to the others here."

Arkad gestured for him to continue, and several voices in the crowd encouraged him as well.

"Well then," the man said, "today I was lucky—I found a purse with gold coins in it. It was a blessing, and I'd like very much to stay lucky. I imagine all of us would. So I propose that we discuss this question: *How can a man attract good luck?* Are there ways to draw it to us?"

Arkad's eyes lit up. "A most interesting subject," he said. "One worthy of our attention."

He continued, "Some men think of good luck as nothing more than blind chance—like a sudden accident that falls into your lap without reason. Others believe that good fortune comes from the hand of the generous goddess Ashtar, who rewards those who win her favor."

He looked around at the group. "So, my friends—what do you think? Shall we try to discover whether there are ways to invite good luck into our lives?"

"*Yes! Yes!*" called out the crowd. "*Let's hear it! Much good luck to all of us!*"

"Then let's begin," Arkad said. "Let's hear first from any man here who, like our cloth weaver, has stumbled upon treasure or received a gift of great value—without effort or expectation."

The room grew quiet. Men looked at each other, waiting. But no one spoke.

"No one?" Arkad asked, raising his eyebrows. "Then perhaps such luck is indeed rare. If that kind of fortune is so uncommon, perhaps we should look elsewhere for answers."

A young man in a fine robe stood up.

"I'll speak," he said. "When we talk about luck, isn't it natural to think of the *gaming tables*—where men hope to win favor from the goddess and walk away with a heavy purse?"

As he sat back down, a voice called out from the other side of the room, teasing:

"Don't stop there! Tell us what happened! Did the goddess favor you? Did the dice roll red, and you took the dealer's gold? Or did they come up blue, and the dealer took your hard-earned silver?"

The young man laughed along with the crowd. "I admit the goddess paid me no attention at all," he said. "But what about the rest of you? Has Lady Luck ever rolled the dice in your favor? We're eager to learn."

"A wise place to start," Arkad agreed. "If we're talking about luck, we can't ignore gambling. Most men like to risk a little silver in hopes of winning a lot of gold."

"That reminds me of yesterday's chariot races," another man called out. "If the goddess visits gaming halls, surely she doesn't skip the track—where gold chariots and foaming horses make the stakes even higher. Tell us, Arkad—did she whisper in your ear to bet on those gray horses from Nineveh? I was right behind you and nearly fell over when I heard your wager. Everyone knows no team in Assyria can outrun our bay horses in a fair race.

"Did the goddess hint that on the final turn the inside black chariot would stumble, block the bays, and let the grays steal the win?"

Arkad smiled at the teasing. "Why should we imagine the good goddess takes such interest in any man's bet? I see her as a dignified helper of those who need—and those who deserve—her aid. I don't expect to meet her at dice tables or racetracks, where men usually lose more gold than they win. I look for her where people do work that truly matters and earns real reward.

"When a man tills his fields, trades honestly, or practices any useful craft, he has a fair chance to profit. Not every time— poor judgment or bad weather can spoil his efforts—but if he keeps at it, the odds favor him.

"At the gaming tables, the odds are reversed. Profit is built into the house—always in favor of the gamekeeper, always against the player. Few realize how certain the house's gains are, and how uncertain their own hope to win.

"Look at a simple dice game. Each cast, you bet on a single red face to land up. If the red comes up, the master pays you four times your wager. But if any of the other five faces show, you lose. So you face **five chances to lose** and only **four**

chances to win, and the gamekeeper knows over many rolls he'll keep about one-fifth of all the silver wagered.

"Can any player expect to come out ahead for long when the odds guarantee he'll lose one coin in every five?"

The young man laughed along with everyone else. "It seems the goddess hardly knew I was there," he admitted. "But what about the rest of you? Has Lady Luck ever singled you out at the gaming tables? We're eager to hear—and to learn."

"Excellent," Arkad said. "We're here to consider every side of a question. Ignoring the dice table would be ignoring a common instinct: the urge to risk a little silver for the chance of a lot of gold."

"That reminds me of yesterday's chariot races," another listener called. "If the goddess likes gaming halls, surely she visits the track—where gold-plated chariots and foaming horses make the stakes even higher. Tell us honestly, Arkad: did she whisper in your ear to bet on those gray horses from Nineveh? I was right behind you and couldn't believe it when you wagered on the grays. Everyone knows no team in Assyria can beat our bay horses in a fair race! Did the goddess warn you the inside black chariot would stumble, block the bays, and let the grays steal the victory?"

Arkad smiled at the teasing. "Why imagine the goddess takes such interest in one man's bet? I picture her as a dignified spirit who helps those in real need and rewards those who deserve it. I don't expect to meet her at dice tables or racetracks, where men usually lose more gold than they win. I look for her where honest work brings honest profit.

"When a man farms his land, trades fairly, or practices a useful craft, the odds favor him. Not every season brings success—poor judgment or bad weather can spoil his efforts—but if he keeps at it, profit usually follows.

"At the gaming tables, the odds run the other way. Profit is built in for the house, loss for the player. Few gamblers realize how sure the keeper's winnings are and how uncertain their own chances."

He gave a quick example: "Take a simple dice game: you bet on one red face. If red lands up, the master pays four times your wager; if any of the other five faces land up, you lose. That's **five chances to lose** versus **four to win**. Over many rolls, the gamekeeper can expect to keep about one-fifth of all coins wagered. How long can a player come out ahead against odds like that?"

A man at the front shrugged. "Yet sometimes people do win big."

"True," Arkad said. "But I wonder—does money won that way bring lasting success? Among all the prosperous men I know in Babylon, not one started his fortune at the gaming tables. You here know many solid citizens. How many of our city's successes began with dice or races? Speak up."

The room fell silent until a wag in the back called, "Should we count the gamekeepers?"

"If you can name no one else," Arkad chuckled.

He waited. No one volunteered. "Then it seems Lady Luck rarely builds real wealth there. So let's look elsewhere. We gain nothing from lost purses, dice, or horses—and I admit I've lost far more at the track than I've ever won."

He scanned the group. "Let's consider our trades and businesses. If we close a profitable deal, we call it fair reward for effort, not luck. Maybe the goddess helps us more than we notice—perhaps she smiles on diligence. Who has another angle?"

When Opportunity Knocks — and We Miss It

An elderly merchant, smoothing his white robe, rose. "With your permission, Arkad, I suggest we talk about *missed* opportunities—those times good fortune brushed our fingertips but slipped away. They're the purest examples of luck: potential profits that never turned into earnings, so we can't claim them as just rewards. I'm sure many here know such stories."

"A wise idea," Arkad said. "Who has had good luck almost within grasp, only to watch it escape?"

Hands went up, including the merchant's. Arkad pointed to him. "You spoke first—let's hear your tale."

The merchant began. "My story shows how near good luck can come, and how blindly a man can let it slip—only to regret it later.

"Years ago, when I was newly married and earning a modest living, my father urged me into an investment. The son of one of his friends had spotted a barren plot of land just outside the city walls—high ground that the canal's water couldn't reach.

"That young man planned to buy the land, build three large ox-powered water wheels, lift water to the soil, divide the acreage into small herb gardens, and sell the plots to city dwellers.

"But he lacked enough gold. Like me, he was earning but modestly. His father, like mine, had a big family and little cash. So the son proposed a partnership of twelve men, each agreeing to invest one-tenth of his earnings until the project was ready. Profits would be shared in proportion to each man's contribution.

"My father said to me: 'My son, you're in your young manhood. Start building a valuable estate now, so you'll be respected in later years. Learn from my mistakes. From your wages, keep one-tenth for sound investments. What that tenth earns will, over time, build you real wealth.'"

"Your words are wise, Father," I replied. "I do long for wealth. But my income is pulled in so many directions. I hesitate to follow your advice. I'm still young—there's plenty of time."

"So I thought when I was your age," he said, shaking his head. "Yet here I am, years later, and I've still not begun."

"We live in different times," I told him. "I won't make your mistakes."

"My son," he said firmly, "opportunity stands before you now. It's offering you a real chance to build wealth. I beg you—don't delay. Go tomorrow to the young man I told you about. Agree to invest one-tenth of your income into his plan. Go tomorrow. Opportunity doesn't wait. Today it is here— tomorrow, it may be gone."

In spite of my father's pleading, I hesitated.

Just that week, traders from the East had arrived with beautiful new robes—robes so rich and finely made that my wife and I felt we *must* have them. But if I were to commit one-tenth of my income to the land venture, we would have to go without those robes… and several other pleasures we desired.

So I delayed.

And by the time I was ready to act, it was too late.

The opportunity had passed—and the investment turned out far more profitable than anyone predicted. To this day, I regret letting that chance slip through my fingers. That is my story—how I let good luck walk away.

The Truth About Luck and Preparedness

"A clear lesson," said a dark-skinned man from the desert. "Good luck comes to the man who seizes opportunity when it knocks. To build wealth, a man must begin. That beginning might be just a few silver coins, set aside from his earnings and put into his first investment. I myself started my herds as a young boy, buying a single calf with one silver piece. That calf became the beginning of my wealth.

"To take that first step—from laboring for every coin to having your money earn for you—is the best kind of luck a man can have. Some take that step early and race ahead in wealth. Others, like the father in our story, never take it at all.

"Had our merchant friend taken that first step when he had the chance, he'd be far richer today. If the cloth weaver's recent stroke of good luck leads him to take such a step now, it could be the beginning of even greater fortune."

The Habit That Attracts Good Fortune
"Thank you," said another man, standing up. His accent was thick. "I would like to speak too. I am a Syrian. I do not speak your tongue so well. I wish to call our friend, the merchant, a name. Maybe you think it not polite. But I want to say it.

"Problem is, I don't know the word in your language. If I say it in Syrian, you will not understand. So—will one of you tell me—what is the word you use for a man who always puts off doing things that would help him?"

From the crowd, a voice called out: **"Procrastinator."**

"That's him!" shouted the Syrian, waving his arms excitedly. "He doesn't accept opportunity when it comes. He waits. He says, 'I have much to do right now. I'll think about it later.' But opportunity won't wait for a slow man! She thinks, 'If a man truly wants to be lucky, he'll act quickly.' A man who won't act when opportunity comes—he's a true procrastinator, just like our merchant friend."

The merchant stood and gave a good-natured bow as laughter spread through the hall. "My admiration to you, stranger in our midst. You don't hesitate to speak the truth!"

"And now," said Arkad, "let's hear another story of opportunity. Who else has an experience to share?"

"I do," said a middle-aged man in a red robe. "I buy animals—mostly camels and horses, sometimes sheep and goats. The story I'll tell is about an opportunity that came to me suddenly one night. Because it was so unexpected, I let it slip away. You be the judge."

"I had just returned from a disappointing ten-day trip in search of camels. I was tired and frustrated, only to find the gates of the city closed and locked for the night. While my slaves set up our camp, expecting a night with little food or water, an elderly farmer approached me. He too was locked out."

"'Sir,' he said, 'you look like a buyer. I have an excellent flock of sheep I must sell immediately. My wife lies very ill with fever, and I must return home at once. Buy my flock so I can leave quickly.'"

"It was too dark to see the flock, but from the sounds, I could tell it was large. The price he asked was quite reasonable, and I was eager to make a deal after my fruitless trip. I agreed, thinking I could bring the sheep into the city at sunrise and make a solid profit."

"The deal made, I called for torches to count the flock—which he claimed numbered 900. But it was impossible to count them in the dark. I told him I'd pay in the morning once we had a proper count."

"'Please, honorable sir,' he begged, 'pay me two-thirds now. I'll leave my most trusted slave to help with the count. You can pay the rest in the morning.'"

"But I was stubborn. I insisted on waiting."

"Next morning, before I even woke up, the city gates opened and four eager buyers rushed out. Because the city was under threat of siege and food was scarce, they were willing to pay a high price. The farmer sold the flock to them—at nearly three times the price he offered me. That was an opportunity lost. A stroke of good luck… slipped right through my fingers."

"A rare and revealing tale," Arkad said. "What lesson does this one offer?"

"The wisdom of acting promptly when a good deal is at hand," said an older saddle maker. "When I know a deal is good, I act—because I know I'm just as likely to talk myself out of it as anyone else is. We humans are strange. When we're wrong, we're stubborn. But when we're right, we often second-guess ourselves. I've learned my first instinct is usually correct. So I've made it a habit to commit right away. A quick deposit protects me from my own doubt—and from the loss of good luck I might otherwise miss."

"Thank you!" said the Syrian, leaping up again. "These stories are the same! Opportunity comes—with a good plan. But they hesitate. They wait. They say, 'Maybe later is better.' How can anyone succeed this way?"

"Wise words, my friend," said the animal buyer. "In both stories, procrastination drove good luck away. And that's not unusual. Procrastination lives inside every man. We say we want success, yet when the chance comes, we delay. We make excuses. I used to think it was poor judgment... then I blamed my stubbornness. But finally, I saw it for what it was—a habit of unnecessary delay, when action was needed. Once I recognized it, I broke free—and it changed my life."

"I want to ask the merchant a question," the Syrian said, turning to him. "You wear fine robes. You speak like a successful man. Tell us—do you still listen when procrastination whispers in your ear?"

"I had to learn to conquer it," the merchant replied. "It was my enemy—always watching, always waiting to block my progress. The story I told is just one of many. I now treat procrastination like a thief. No man lets a thief steal from his house, and I don't let procrastination steal my opportunities. Once I recognized its danger, I beat it. Every man must do the same if he wants a share of Babylon's riches."

"What say you, Arkad?" he added. "Many call you the luckiest man in Babylon. But surely no man can find true success until he crushes procrastination?"

"You're absolutely right," Arkad replied. "I've watched generations walk the road of trade, learning, and opportunity. Some grasped the chances before them and moved forward to fulfill their dreams. But most... they hesitated. They doubted. They delayed. And they fell behind."

Arkad turned to the cloth weaver. "You asked us to talk about good luck. What do you think of it now?"

"I see it differently," the weaver said. "I used to think of luck as something that just happened to a man. But now I understand—luck doesn't just fall from the sky. It comes when we accept opportunity. From now on, I'll try to act quickly when a good opportunity comes my way."

The Final Word: Luck Comes to Those Who Act
"Well said," Arkad nodded. "We set out tonight to discover how to attract good luck—and I believe we have found the answer. In both stories, luck followed opportunity. And here is the lesson, my friends. A truth that no number of tales, won or lost, can change: **Good luck can be attracted by accepting opportunity.**

Those who are eager to improve themselves—who act quickly when opportunity knocks—draw the favor of the good goddess. She delights in helping those who take action. Action leads you toward the success you seek.

Men of action are favored by the Goddess of Good Luck.

The Five Laws of Gold

*"A bag heavy with gold… or a tablet inscribed
with wisdom. If you had to choose, which would
you take?"*

By the flickering light of the desert fire, the sun-weathered
faces around the circle glowed with curiosity.

"The gold! The gold!" came the enthusiastic chorus of all
twenty-seven young men.

Old Kalabab smiled knowingly. "Listen," he said, raising a
hand. "Do you hear the wild dogs out in the dark? They howl
and cry because they are thin with hunger. But feed them—
and what do they do? Fight and strut about, thinking only of
the moment. They give no thought to the hunger that will
come again tomorrow."

"So it is with men," he continued. "Offer them a choice
between gold and wisdom, and what do they choose? The
gold. Always the gold. They ignore the wisdom, waste the
gold, and then cry the next day because they have nothing
left."

"But gold," he said with conviction, "belongs to those who
understand its rules and live by them."

Kalabab pulled his white robe tighter around his legs as a cool
wind swept across the desert.

The Lesson Begins

"Because you've served me faithfully—because you cared for my camels with diligence, because you endured the burning sands without complaint, and because you stood bravely against the robbers who tried to steal from me—I will tell you tonight a story worth more than all the gold I carry. It is the story of the *Five Laws of Gold*. And if you truly understand and live by these laws, your future will be filled with abundance."

He paused, letting the silence stretch.

Above them, the stars shimmered like diamonds in the crisp night sky. Behind the group, their worn tents flapped softly in the breeze, securely staked against the shifting sands. Stacks of merchandise lay protected under animal hides, and not far off, their camels rested—some lazily chewing their cud, others snoring with deep, rumbling grunts.

"You've told us many good stories, Kalabab," said the chief packer. "We look to your wisdom to guide us tomorrow, when our service with you comes to an end."

"I've only told you of my travels in strange and distant lands," Kalabab replied. "But tonight, I'll share the wisdom of Arkad—the richest man in Babylon."

"We've heard much about him," said the chief packer. "They say he was the wealthiest man who ever lived in Babylon."

"And rightly so," Kalabab nodded. "He was the richest because he understood the ways of gold better than any man before or after him. Tonight, I will share the great wisdom he passed down—wisdom I heard from his son, Nomasir, many years ago in Nineveh, back when I was just a boy.

A Father's Test

"My master and I had been at Nomasir's palace late into the night. We had brought him bundles of the finest rugs—each one unrolled and examined until he found the colors that pleased him most. When he was satisfied, he invited us to sit with him and drink a rare, fragrant wine. It was strong, and I wasn't used to it—it warmed my belly more than anything I'd ever tasted.

"Then Nomasir began to tell us the story of his father's wisdom, and now I will pass it on to you.

"In Babylon, as you know, it's the custom for the sons of wealthy men to live with their fathers, waiting to inherit the family fortune. But Arkad didn't agree with that. So, when Nomasir came of age, Arkad called him in and said:

'My son, it is my desire that you inherit my estate. But first, you must prove that you are worthy of it—that you can handle it wisely. That means going out into the world and showing that you can not only earn gold but also earn respect.

'To help you begin, I will give you two things—two things I myself did not have when I started out as a poor young man.

'First, I give you this bag of gold. If you use it wisely, it can become the foundation of your future success.

'Second, I give you this clay tablet on which are written the Five Laws of Gold. If you apply them to your life, they will bring you wealth and security.

'Now go. Ten years from today, return to my house and tell me what you've done. If you've proven yourself, I will name you my heir. But if not, I will give all that I own to the priests, so they may barter with the gods on behalf of my soul.'"

So Nomasir left Babylon to make his own way in the world. He took with him the bag of gold, the clay tablet inscribed with the Five Laws of Gold, a trusted servant, and a pair of horses for their journey.

Ten years passed. As promised, Nomasir returned to his father's house. Arkad prepared a great feast in his honor and invited many friends and family members to celebrate the homecoming. After the meal, Arkad and his wife sat on elevated seats in the great hall, and Nomasir stood before them to give an account of his journey and what he had learned.

It was evening, and the room was dim, lit only by the flickering light of oil lamps. The air was heavy with the smell of smoke, and slaves fanned the guests with long palm leaves. A dignified hush fell over the room. Nomasir's wife and sons sat behind him on rugs, along with other family and friends, eager to hear his report.

"My father," Nomasir began with respect, "I bow to your wisdom. Ten years ago, when I stood at the edge of manhood, you challenged me to go out into the world and prove myself—to earn my own success rather than rely on your wealth.

"You gave me gold—generously. You gave me wisdom—freely. And I must admit, the gold quickly slipped through my inexperienced fingers.

I lost it all."

Arkad smiled knowingly. "Go on, my son. Your story intrigues me."

"I decided to travel to Nineveh, a growing city where I believed opportunities would be abundant. I joined a caravan, and along the way, I made many new friends. Two men in particular caught my attention—they spoke well and owned a magnificent white horse, fast as the wind.

"During our journey, they confided in me. They said that in Nineveh there was a wealthy man who owned a horse he believed to be unbeatable. He was so confident that he would bet any amount that his horse could outrun any other in Babylon.

"My new companions offered to let me in on what they claimed was a sure bet. They said their white horse was much faster and couldn't lose. I believed them. I joined in the wager.

"But their horse lost badly—and with it, I lost a large portion of my gold. Later I learned it was all a scam. The so-called unbeatable horse belonged to their partner, and the three of them were running this scheme on every caravan that passed through. That was my first painful lesson in being cautious with whom I trust—and in guarding my gold more carefully.

"But I wasn't done learning the hard way.

"Soon after arriving in Nineveh, I became close friends with another young man, the son of wealthy parents, also there to seek opportunity. He told me about a merchant who had died, leaving behind a valuable shop full of inventory and loyal customers. The shop could supposedly be purchased for a very low price.

"He proposed that we go into business together as equal partners. But he didn't have his gold with him and said he needed to return to Babylon to get it. In the meantime, he urged me to use my gold to buy the store and inventory.

"I agreed. But he delayed his trip home again and again. Worse, he turned out to be reckless with spending and had no business sense. Eventually, I had to cut ties with him—but by then, the store was failing, the inventory was worthless, and I had no money left to restock.

"In the end, I sold the remains to a traveling Israelite for a small fraction of what I had paid. That was the end of my gold."

"Soon after that," Nomasir continued, "came hard, bitter days. I looked everywhere for work—but no one would hire me. I had no skill or trade to offer that could earn an income. I sold my horses. I sold my servant. I even sold my extra robes, just to afford food and shelter. But every day, the shadow of poverty crept closer.

"And yet, Father, in those darkest days, I remembered your faith in me. You had sent me out into the world to become a man—and I was determined not to fail you."

At this, Nomasir's mother wept quietly, burying her face in her hands.

"It was then that I remembered the clay tablet you had given me—the one with the Five Laws of Gold carved into it. I pulled it out and read your words again, this time with care and determination. That was when I understood the truth: if I had only sought wisdom before trying to use gold, I never would have lost it all.

"I memorized each law. I made a vow that if ever the goddess of good fortune smiled on me again, I would follow the guidance of wisdom, not the mistakes of youth.

The Five Laws of Gold
"And now, for the benefit of everyone gathered here tonight, I will read the Five Laws of Gold, just as they were engraved on the clay tablet you gave me ten years ago."

1. Gold comes easily and grows steadily for any man who sets aside at least one-tenth of his income to build a future for himself and his family.
2. Gold works hard and faithfully for the wise owner who finds smart and profitable uses for it. Like livestock in the field, it multiplies when well employed.
3. Gold stays safe in the hands of the cautious investor who puts it only into ventures recommended by experienced and trustworthy advisors.

4. Gold slips away from the man who invests in things he doesn't understand or into ventures that are not trusted by those who know money well.

5. Gold runs from the man who tries to make it earn unrealistic returns, who follows the tempting advice of dishonest schemers, or who trusts his money to his own inexperience and wishful thinking.

"These," Nomasir said, holding up the tablet, "are the Five Laws of Gold, written by my father. And I declare they are more valuable than gold itself—as I will now show by the rest of my story."

The Turning Point
He turned again to face his father. "I have told you how far I fell—into poverty and despair—because of my lack of experience.

"But no season of hardship lasts forever. Mine came to an end when I found work overseeing a crew of slaves who were building the new outer wall of the city.

"Remembering the first law of gold, I saved a small copper coin from my first wages. I added to it every chance I had until I held a piece of silver. It was slow work, for I still had to live—but I spent cautiously and with purpose. I had set my heart on replacing the gold you gave me before the ten years were up.

"One day, the overseer of the slaves, who had become my friend, said to me, 'You're a careful young man who doesn't waste his wages. Have you saved any gold that's just sitting idle?'

"'Yes,' I said. 'More than anything, I want to rebuild what my father once gave me and which I foolishly lost.'

"'That's a worthy goal,' he said. 'But do you know that your gold can go to work for you—and earn even more gold?'

"'I want to believe that,' I said. 'But my past experience has made me cautious. I'm afraid of losing the little I've managed to save.'"

The overseer smiled. "If you trust me, I'll show you how gold can work for you," he said. "Within a year, the new outer wall will be finished, and the city will need massive bronze gates for every entrance. But there isn't enough metal in all of Nineveh, and the king hasn't prepared for it.

"Here's my plan: a few of us will pool our gold, send a caravan to the distant copper and tin mines, and bring back the metal ourselves. When the king commands, 'Build the great gates,' we alone will have the supply—and he'll pay a rich price. And if, for some reason, the king refuses, the metal itself can still be sold for a solid profit."

I recognized an opportunity to follow the **Third Law of Gold**—invest under the guidance of men experienced in money. I joined them, and the venture was a success. My modest savings multiplied.

In time, they invited me into other ventures. These men were cautious and wise: every proposal was debated thoroughly. They avoided any deal that might endanger their capital or trap their money. Foolish bets—like my ill-fated horse race or that disastrous partnership—would never have survived their scrutiny.

From them, I learned to invest safely and profitably. Year by year, my treasure grew—first recouping my losses, then far surpassing them.

Through setbacks, trials, and eventual success, I tested the **Five Laws of Gold** over and over, proving them true.

Without knowledge of the laws, gold seldom comes, and quickly leaves.

With the laws, gold arrives—and serves its owner faithfully.

A Son Returns with Wealth

Nomasir paused and gestured to a servant. The man brought forward three heavy leather bags. Nomasir placed the first at his father's feet.

"Father, you once gave me a bag of Babylonian gold. In its place, I return a bag of Nineveh gold—equal in weight, an equal exchange.

"You also gave me a clay tablet carved with wisdom." He set the other two bags beside the first. "In its place, I return not one, but **two** bags of gold. Let this show how much more I value your wisdom than the gold itself.

"For without wisdom, gold quickly slips away. With wisdom, anyone—even one who has lost everything—can earn it back, as these three bags prove.

"It brings me great joy to say that, because of your teachings, I am now wealthy and respected."

Arkad laid a fond hand on his son's head. "You have learned your lessons well, my son. I am fortunate to have someone so worthy to inherit my estate."

Kalabab's Final Charge

Kalabab finished his tale and looked around, measuring the faces of his listeners in the firelight.

"What does Nomasir's story mean to **you**?" he asked. "Could any of you walk up to your father—or your father-in-law—and give an account of how wisely you've handled your earnings?

"Would the old men be pleased if you said, *'I've traveled, I've worked hard, I've earned a lot—yet I have almost no gold. Some I spent wisely, some foolishly, and much I lost in bad deals.'* "If you still believe it's mere fate that makes some men rich while others stay poor, you're mistaken.

"Rich men simply **know** the Five Laws of Gold—and live by them."

He drew his robe tighter against the night breeze. "I, too, learned those laws when I was young. Because I followed them year after year, I became a wealthy merchant. Wealth that arrives overnight disappears the same way. Wealth that stays—wealth that brings pride and comfort—grows slowly, born of knowledge and steady purpose."

He paused. "The Five Laws reward anyone who keeps them. Each law is short, but each is packed with meaning. Listen again—and remember them word for word."

The First Law

Gold comes gladly and grows steadily for the person who saves at least one-tenth of every coin he earns, building a future for himself and his family.

"Save a tenth of everything you make, invest it wisely, and you'll create an estate that cares for you and protects your loved ones. I've proved this myself: the more gold I save, the faster more gold finds me. Your savings earn more—and those earnings earn still more. That is the First Law at work."

The Second Law

Gold works hard and happily for the wise owner who finds profitable uses for it, multiplying like the flocks of the field.

"Gold is a tireless worker. Give it a good job and watch it grow. Once you have a store of gold, worthwhile opportunities will come—and over the years that gold will multiply in surprising ways."

The Third Law

Gold stays safe with the cautious investor who seeks advice from those skilled in handling money.

"Gold clings to careful hands and flees the careless. A man who listens to experienced financiers soon learns to keep his capital safe and enjoy steady growth."

The Fourth Law
Gold slips away from anyone who invests in businesses or schemes he doesn't understand, or that are not approved by wise advisers.

"To the untrained eye, many plans look profitable. But once examined by experts, most prove risky or unsound. Trusting your own guesswork in an unfamiliar field is the surest way to watch gold disappear."

The Fifth Law
Gold runs from the man who tries to force it to impossible returns, who follows the tempting words of swindlers, or who lets greed and fantasy guide his investments.

"Dazzling offers that read like adventure stories flock to the new owner of gold. Wise men know the dangers hiding behind promises of rapid riches. Remember the shrewd traders of Nineveh: they would never risk losing their principal or lock it in dead-end ventures."

Final Words by the Fire
"That ends my tale," Kalabab said. "These are not secrets—only truths every man must master if he wishes to rise above the pack that struggles each day just to eat.

"Look!" He pointed toward the horizon where a steady flame glowed in the night. "The sacred fire above the Temple of Bel. By tomorrow we'll be inside Babylon's golden walls.

"Tomorrow each of you will receive the gold you have earned on this long journey. Ten years from tonight, what story will you tell about that gold?

"If even one of you follows Nomasir's example—saves a part of his income and lets the Five Laws guide him—then ten years hence he will be wealthy and respected."

Kalabab's eyes swept the circle.

"Wise choices travel beside us through life, bringing help and happiness; foolish choices chase us, plaguing us with regret—especially the memory of opportunities we let slip away.

"Babylon's treasures grow richer every year. They await men of purpose who claim their rightful share. In your own strong desires there is a magic power. Steer that power with the Five Laws of Gold, and you, too, will share in the endless treasures of Babylon."

The Gold Lender of Babylon

A Spearmaker's Windfall

Fifty pieces of gold! Rodan, a spearmaker of old Babylon, had never before carried so much money in his leather pouch. He walked cheerfully down the King's Highway, fresh from the palace of His most generous Majesty. With each step, the gold jingled at his side—the sweetest sound he had ever heard.

Fifty pieces of gold—all his! He could barely believe his luck. What power lay in those glittering coins! They could buy almost anything: a beautiful home, land, livestock, camels, horses, chariots—whatever his heart desired.

What should he do with it?

That evening, as he turned down a narrow street toward his sister's house, he couldn't think of anything he wanted more than to simply **keep** those shiny, heavy coins. They were his. That alone was enough.

Seeking Counsel, Not Coins

A few days later, Rodan appeared at the workshop of Mathon, Babylon's well-known moneylender and merchant of rare jewels and fine goods. Ignoring the displays of colorful fabrics and expensive wares, he walked straight through to the living quarters in the back.

There, he found Mathon reclining comfortably on a rug, enjoying a meal served by a dark-skinned servant.

Rodan stood firm and serious—feet planted wide, his muscular chest visible through the open front of his leather tunic. "I need your counsel," he said. "I'm unsure what to do."

Mathon's narrow face lit up with a smile. "What's this? Rodan the spearmaker asking the gold lender for **advice**? Did you lose money gambling? Or is some beautiful woman causing you trouble? I've known you for years, but this is the first time you've come to me like this."

Rodan shook his head. "No, no—it's nothing like that. I'm not here to borrow gold. I'm here because I value your wisdom."

Mathon laughed with delight. "Listen to this! My ears must be playing tricks. No one comes to the moneylender for advice. Everyone wants gold, not guidance!"

"I'm serious. I need direction."

"Well then," Mathon said, sitting up with interest, "Rodan the spearmaker must be wiser than most. Many come here to borrow for their foolish mistakes—but rarely does anyone come asking how to avoid them."

He clapped his hands. "Tonight, you are my guest! Andol!" he called to the servant, "bring an extra rug for my friend Rodan, who comes not for gold, but for advice. Bring him a feast and fetch my largest cup. Choose the finest wine—we're going to enjoy this conversation."

"Now, tell me what's troubling you," Mathon said.

"It's the king's gift," Rodan replied.

"The king gave you a gift—and it's causing you trouble? What kind of gift?"

"He was very pleased with the new spearhead design I made for the royal guard, so he rewarded me with fifty pieces of gold. And now... I don't know what to do."

Mathon raised an eyebrow. "Ah. I see. And now that the sun has barely had time to cross the sky, people are already lining up to ask you for a share?"

Rodan nodded. "Yes. All day long, people are trying to get a piece of it."

"That's only natural. More men want gold than have it. And they always hope that someone who comes into it easily will share. But can't you just say no? Isn't your will as strong as your arm?"

"To most of them, yes, I can say no. But sometimes it would honestly be easier to say yes—especially to my sister. I love her dearly. How can I refuse her?"

"She's asked for some of your gold?"

"It's not for her, but for her husband, Araman. She wants him to become a successful merchant. She believes he's never really had a fair chance. She begs me to loan him this gold so he can finally prove himself and pay me back from the profits."

Mathon leaned in thoughtfully. "My friend, this is a good and important question. You see, gold brings more than wealth—it brings responsibility and changes your relationship with others. It makes you fearful you might lose it. It also gives you a sense of power, even the ability to do good. But be careful. Even your best intentions can lead you into trouble.

"Have you ever heard the story of the farmer from Nineveh who could understand the language of animals?"

Rodan shook his head.

"No? I didn't think so. It's not the sort of tale told in the busy forges. But you should hear it—because lending and borrowing involves more than just passing gold from one hand to another.

"This farmer, gifted by the gods, could understand the speech of animals. Each evening, he'd stay out in the yard just to listen to them talk. One night, he heard the ox complaining to the donkey.

"'All day long I plow in the hot sun. My legs ache, my neck is sore from the yoke, and I work until nightfall. But you, my friend—you wear a soft blanket and only carry our master around when he feels like riding. The rest of the time, you eat grass and relax.'

"The donkey, despite his nasty kick, had a kind heart and replied, 'My friend, I see your pain. Let me help you rest. Tomorrow morning, when the servant comes to take you to the field, just lie down and groan. Make it sound like you're sick so they won't make you work.'

"So the next morning, the ox pretended to be sick. When the servant saw this, he reported it to the farmer.

"'Then hitch the donkey to the plow,' said the farmer, 'because the work still needs to be done.'

"All day long, the poor donkey worked in the ox's place. When evening finally came, he was exhausted. His legs trembled, his neck was chafed, and he was in a foul mood.

"The farmer lingered again in the yard to hear what they'd say.

"'You are a good friend,' said the ox, happily. 'Thanks to your advice, I had a wonderful day off.'

"'And I,' snapped the donkey, 'am like many well-meaning fools who try to help a friend, only to end up stuck doing their work. From now on, pull your own plow! I heard the master say that if you're sick again, he'll send for the butcher. I hope he does—you lazy beast!'

"And that ended their friendship. They never spoke again." Mathon leaned back. "So, Rodan, can you guess the moral of the story?"

Rodan frowned. "It's a good story, but... no, I don't see it."

"I figured as much. It's simple: If you want to help a friend, do it in a way that doesn't make **you** carry **his** burdens."

Rodan nodded slowly. "That makes sense. I don't want to end up carrying my brother-in-law's burdens. But tell me something. You lend to many people—don't they pay you back?"

Mathon smiled with the kind of wisdom that only comes from long experience. "Would I make a loan if I knew the borrower couldn't repay? A smart lender must judge whether the gold will be put to good use and whether it will return—or whether it will be wasted by someone who doesn't know what to do with it. Otherwise, I lose my treasure, and they're left with a debt they can't repay.

The Chest of Tokens
"Come. Let me show you something."

He stood and motioned toward a chest in the corner. "I'll show you the tokens I keep in this chest—and the stories they tell will teach you more than I ever could with words alone."

Mathon rose and brought out a long chest—about the length of his arm—covered in red leather and decorated with bronze accents. He set it on the floor and knelt before it, placing both hands on the lid.

"From everyone I lend to," he explained, "I keep a token in this chest. When they repay me, I return it. But if they never repay, the token remains—a reminder that they didn't honor the trust I placed in them."

He tapped the lid thoughtfully.

"This chest has taught me that the safest loans are those backed by property—people who already own land, livestock, jewels, or other assets that could be sold to repay me. Some tokens represent valuable collateral—things worth more than the loan itself. Others are legal promises that say if the loan isn't repaid, I get certain property in return. With those, I sleep well, knowing the loan is secure.

"There's another group—people who don't have property but have the ability to earn. Like you, Rodan. You work, you get paid, and if you're responsible and avoid misfortune, you can repay a loan and even pay interest on it. That kind of loan is based on a man's ability to earn.

"Then, there are the riskiest borrowers—those with no property and no steady income. Life is hard for them. They struggle to keep up. Even if I loan them just a few coins, this chest reminds me later: that gold may never come back. Unless their loan is guaranteed by a trusted friend, I consider it a loss before it leaves my hand."

He unlatched the chest and opened the lid. Rodan leaned forward eagerly.

At the top, nestled on a red cloth, lay a bronze necklace. Mathon picked it up and ran his fingers over it gently.

"This will always stay in the chest. The man who gave me this is gone now. He was my good friend. We did business together for years and had great success. Then one day, he brought a woman from the East—a dazzling beauty, unlike the women of our city. He spent his gold like water to please her every whim.

"When he ran out of money, he came to me in desperation. I tried to help him regain control of his finances. He swore, by the sign of the Great Bull, that he would. But it ended in tragedy. In a heated argument, she stabbed him in the heart with a dagger. He dared her, and she did."

Rodan's eyes widened. "And her?"

Mathon held up the red cloth. "She was overcome with guilt and threw herself into the Euphrates. These two tokens—his necklace and her cloth—will never be redeemed. This chest reminds me that people driven by strong emotion are not safe bets for lending gold."

He set them aside and reached deeper. "Now this one," he said, holding up a simple ring carved from ox bone, "is a different story. It belongs to a farmer. I buy rugs from his family. One year, locusts destroyed his crops and they had no food. I helped him through that winter, and when the next harvest came, he paid me back in full.

"Later, he came again, excited about a new kind of goat he had heard about—one with long, silky hair perfect for weaving beautiful rugs. He wanted to travel and bring back a herd, but needed funding. I loaned him the gold, and now he's building a herd. Next year, I'll surprise the nobles of Babylon with rugs more beautiful than they've ever seen. And he'll repay me—he always insists on paying on time."

Rodan looked impressed. "Do many borrowers repay like that?"

Mathon nodded. "If they borrow for something that will make them money, yes. But if they borrow because they've made foolish choices, be careful—your gold may not come back."

Rodan reached in and picked up a heavy gold bracelet inlaid with rare gemstones.

"What about this one?" he asked.

Mathon laughed. "Ah! The women always catch your eye, don't they?"

Rodan grinned. "I'm still younger than you."

"I'll give you that—but this time, romance is not part of the story. The owner is an older woman, wrinkled and endlessly talkative. She and her husband once had wealth and were regular customers. But hard times came. She wants her son to become a merchant, so she borrowed gold for him to join a caravan trader.

"Unfortunately, the caravan leader turned out to be a con man. He abandoned the boy in a distant city, taking the goods and leaving him with nothing. Maybe someday the boy will grow up and repay me, but for now, I receive no interest on this loan—just long-winded stories.

"To be fair, the jewels are worth the amount she borrowed."

"Did she ask for your advice before taking the loan?" Rodan asked.

"Advice? No. She had already imagined her son becoming a rich and powerful man in Babylon. When I dared to question the plan, she grew furious. I saw the risks clearly—the boy had no experience—but she offered collateral, so I agreed.

Still, it was not a wise loan."

Mathon picked up a short piece of knotted rope.

"This," he said, holding it up, "belongs to Nebatur the camel trader. When he wants to buy a larger herd than he can afford, he brings me this knot as his token, and I lend him what he needs. He's smart—always careful with money. I trust his judgment completely. I have many merchants like him—men whose honesty and wisdom make them good for business.

"Their tokens come and go regularly from this box. Helping them keeps trade moving and makes Babylon stronger. And it profits me, too."

Mathon reached into the chest, pulled out a turquoise beetle pendant, and tossed it onto the rug with disgust.

"A bug from Egypt," he said. "The young man who left this here cares nothing about repaying me. When I remind him of his debt, he shrugs and says, 'Bad luck hounds me—and besides, you have plenty of gold.' What can I do?

"His token was pledged by his father—a decent man of modest means who put up his land and herd to back his son's ventures. The young man found success at first, but got greedy. In his rush for riches, his schemes collapsed.

"You see, youth is ambitious—always looking for shortcuts to wealth. Young men borrow quickly, never realizing that debt can be a deep pit. You can slide in overnight, but you may claw at the walls for years trying to get out. Debt brings sorrow and regret; it turns sunny days gray and keeps you awake at night.

"Even so, I don't dislike lending. I encourage borrowing **when the purpose is wise.** My own first success came from borrowed gold. But a lender must judge carefully. If a borrower is trapped in despair, he'll never repay. And my heart recoils at the thought of taking his father's land and cattle to settle the debt."

Should Love Trump Judgment

Rodan nodded thoughtfully. "You've told me many interesting things, but you still haven't answered my question: Should I lend my fifty pieces of gold to my sister's husband? They mean a great deal to me."

Mathon sat forward. "Your sister is a fine woman—I esteem her greatly. If her husband came to me for fifty pieces of gold, my first question would be: *For what purpose?*

"Suppose he said, 'I want to become a merchant like you— trading in jewels and fine furnishings.' I'd ask, 'What do you know of the trade? Do you know where to buy at the best price? Do you know where to sell at a fair price?' Could he answer yes?"

Rodan shook his head. "No. He helps me make spears, and he's done a little work in various shops, but that's it."

"Then I'd tell him his plan isn't wise. A merchant must learn his trade. His ambition may be noble, but it isn't practical—and I wouldn't lend him a single coin.

"But imagine he said: 'Yes, I've spent years helping caravan merchants. I know how to travel to Smyrna and buy rugs directly from the weavers at low cost. I also know wealthy families in Babylon who'll pay top price for those rugs.' Then I'd say, 'Your plan is sound and your ambition realistic. I'll gladly lend you the fifty pieces—*if* you can offer security to guarantee repayment.'

"Now suppose he said, 'I have no collateral, but I'm an honorable man and will pay you well for the loan.' I'd answer: 'I treasure every piece of gold. If bandits rob you on the way to Smyrna, or thieves steal your rugs on the way back, you'll have no way to repay me—and my gold will be gone.'

"Gold is a money-lender's merchandise. It is easy to hand out; it is hard to get back if the loan is foolish. A wise lender wants certainty of repayment, not the thrill of risk.

"It is good," Mathon added, "to help those in trouble, to assist people burdened by fate, and to give newcomers a start so they can become valuable citizens. But help must be given wisely—otherwise, like the helpful donkey in the farmer's tale, we end up carrying someone else's load."

He looked Rodan in the eye. "So here is my answer: **Keep your fifty pieces of gold.** What you've earned through sweat and what the king rewarded you with is yours alone. No one can claim it unless you wish it. If you do lend it, make sure it earns more gold—lend cautiously, spread your risk, and never let your money sit idle, but avoid reckless ventures."

Mathon thought a moment. "Tell me, Rodan—how many years have you worked as a spearmaker?"

"Three," Rodan said.

"And besides the king's gift, how much have you managed to save?"

"Three gold pieces."

"So, each year, through hard work and self-denial, you've saved exactly one piece of gold?"

"It's as you say."

"Then at that rate, it would take you **fifty years**—a lifetime of labor—to save fifty pieces of gold on your own."

Rodan nodded.

"Do you think your sister would want to jeopardize the savings of fifty years of work just so her husband can *experiment* at being a merchant?"

"Not if I explained it the way you have."

"Then go to her," Mathon advised, "and say:

'For three long years I have labored—every day but holy days—from dawn until dusk. I have denied myself many pleasures my heart desired. Each year of sacrifice has earned me one single piece of gold. You are my beloved sister, and I wish your husband every success. If he can show me a plan that seems sound to Mathon, the wisest money-lender in Babylon, then I will gladly lend him *one* year's savings—one piece of gold—to prove himself.'

"Do this, my friend, and you will help your sister without risking the treasure that took you a lifetime to earn."

"Follow that plan," Mathon said, "and if your brother-in-law truly has what it takes, he can prove it with a single piece of gold. If he fails, he'll owe you no more than he can reasonably repay."

He leaned forward. "I lend gold because I have more than I can use in my own trade. I want my surplus to *work* for others and bring me a fair return. But I refuse to take foolish risks. I earned my gold through long toil and self-denial, and I won't lend it unless I'm convinced it is safe *and* that its earnings will come back on time."

Better a Little Caution

Mathon tapped the open chest. "The tokens you've seen tonight reveal both the weakness and the eagerness of men. Many borrow in hopes of great profit—but most lack the skill or training to achieve it. High hopes are often false hopes."

He fixed Rodan with a steady gaze. "You now possess gold. Handle it wisely and it will earn more for you, becoming a source of pleasure and profit all your life. Let it slip away, and it will haunt you with regret."

"What do you want most from the gold in your pouch?" Mathon asked.

"To keep it safe," Rodan replied.

"A good first desire," Mathon said, nodding. "Would it truly be safe in your brother-in-law's hands?"

"I'm afraid not. He isn't careful with money."

"Then don't let sentiment overrule judgment. If you want to help family, find ways that don't endanger your treasure. Gold disappears quickly when guarded by the careless."

Mathon raised a second finger. "After safety, what next?"

"I want it to earn more gold."

"Again—wise. Properly lent, your fifty pieces could double before you reach old age. But if you risk losing it, you lose not only the capital but all the earnings it might have made.

"Beware of grand schemes promising impossible returns. Those are dreams spun by people who don't understand sound trade. Expect moderate, reliable gains. Partner with men and businesses whose success is already proven. Let their skill work for you and protect your investment."

Mathon closed the chest. "The king's gift will teach you much, Rodan. Many tempting offers will come, plenty of advice— good and bad—will reach your ears. Remember the stories from my token box: before you let a single coin leave your pouch, be sure you have a *safe* way to bring it back again. If you ever want more guidance, return—I'll gladly share what I know.

"And before you go," he added, lifting the lid one last time, "read the words I carved beneath it. They apply to borrowers and lenders alike."

Rodan peered inside and saw the inscription:

BETTER A LITTLE CAUTION
THAN A GREAT REGRET

He nodded, closed his wallet of fifty gold pieces, and left Mathon's house determined to guard his treasure with wisdom—and lend it only where safety and steady gain were certain.

The Walls of Babylon

The Siege Begins

Old Banzar, a grizzled warrior from another era, stood watch at the passage leading to the top of Babylon's massive outer wall. Above him, brave soldiers fought to defend the city. The fate of Babylon—its hundreds of thousands of citizens—depended on those walls holding firm.

From the other side came the noise of war: the shouting of enemy troops, the thunder of horses, and the bone-shaking slam of battering rams pounding the great bronze gates.

Just inside those gates stood a small unit of spearmen, ready to defend should the gates fall. They were too few. The main Babylonian army, led by the king, was far away on campaign in the East. No one had expected an invasion during their absence.

But now, from the north, the Assyrian army had descended—swift, massive, and violent. And Babylon would either stand behind its walls… or fall.

Citizens swarmed around Banzar in fear. Pale and panicked, they begged for news. Each time another wounded or dying defender was carried down the passage, they gasped and whispered.

This gate had become the enemy's main focus. After three days of circling the city, they had concentrated all their might here.

From above, Babylon's defenders fought back with arrows, boiling oil, and their own blood. And from below, the enemy's archers rained down death in return.

Banzar was closest to the fight. He heard the news first. He stood firm.

An old merchant approached, hands shaking with fear.

"Please! Tell me! They're not getting in, are they? My sons are with the king. No one's left to protect my wife. They'll steal everything—our food, our lives. We're too old to run, too old to fight. We'll die. Tell me the walls will hold!"

"Calm yourself," Banzar answered with steady strength. "The walls of Babylon are strong. Go home. Tell your wife that these walls will guard you just as they guard the treasures of the king. But keep close to the buildings—arrows fly over the top."

The old man backed away as a woman stepped forward, holding a baby in her arms.

"Sergeant," she whispered, "please—my husband lies wounded with fever, but still insists on putting on his armor to protect me and the child in my womb. He says the enemy will show no mercy if they break through."

Banzar's eyes softened. "Take heart, mother. The walls will protect you, your husband, and the child you carry. They're high. They're strong. Do you not hear the war cries of our defenders, pouring burning oil on the ladders as they climb?"

"I hear the oil," she said. "And the battering rams slamming into the gates."

"Then tell your husband the gates are holding, and the men who climb the walls fall to waiting spears. Now go—stay close to the walls and out of the open."

Banzar stepped aside as fresh troops marched past—armor clanking, shields shining. A little girl tugged on his belt.

"Soldier," she said, voice trembling, "are we safe? I hear the shouting. I see the bleeding men. I'm scared. What will happen to us? To my mother? My little brother? The baby?"

Banzar blinked, then leaned down. "Be brave, little one. The walls of Babylon will protect you all. That's why Queen Semiramis built them over a hundred years ago—to keep children like you safe. No enemy has ever broken through them. Go tell your mother: You are safe."

And so he stood—day after day—as the wounded came down and the fresh fighters went up. The blood-soaked passage behind him turned to mud beneath the marching feet. But still, the people came, asking the same question.

And every time, Banzar gave them the same answer:

"The walls of Babylon will protect you."

The Walls Hold

The siege dragged on—three weeks and five days of unrelenting assault. But on the night of the fourth week, something changed. The sounds of battle faded. As the sun rose, it revealed a dust cloud—enemy troops retreating.

Cheers erupted. The defenders roared in victory. The streets exploded with joy. The Temple of Bel lit a great fire on its highest tower, sending smoke high into the sky as a signal of triumph.

Babylon had held firm.

Once more, her walls had stood strong against a violent enemy seeking her gold, her people, her soul.

For centuries, Babylon stood—not by luck, but by **preparation**. She was strong because she had made herself strong.

The towering walls of Babylon are a symbol of mankind's need for **protection**. That need is as real today as it was then.

Today, we build different walls—**insurance policies, savings accounts, dependable investments**. These guard us from the unforeseen disasters that can storm into any life without warning.

We cannot afford to live without protection.

Just like Babylon, we survive by what we prepare.

The Camel Trader of Babylon

When a man is truly hungry, his mind sharpens—and his nose can catch even the faintest whiff of food.

Tarkad, son of Azure, felt that in every aching bone. For two days he had eaten nothing but two small figs he'd snatched from a garden. Before he could swipe a third, the owner chased him off, her angry shrieks still ringing in his ears as he wandered through Babylon's market. Those shouts were the only thing that kept his hands from stealing the tempting fruit piled high in the vendors' baskets.

He'd never noticed before how much food flooded into Babylon's stalls—or how incredible it smelled. Leaving the market, he drifted toward a busy inn, pacing back and forth in front of its doorway. Maybe he'd spot someone he knew—someone who might lend him a copper. A single coin would buy him a friendly nod from the innkeeper and, with luck, a generous meal. Without it, he knew he'd be shoved aside.

Lost in thought, Tarkad suddenly found himself face-to-face with the one man he most hoped to avoid: Dabasir the camel trader—tall, lean, and not easily fooled. Of all the people Tarkad owed, Dabasir was the one whose debts pinched most; he'd broken too many promises to repay this man.

Dabasir's eyes lit up. "Ah! Tarkad—the very fellow I've been hunting! You remember the two copper coins I lent you last month? And the silver piece before that? I could use them today. Well, boy, what say you?"

Tarkad's cheeks burned. Weak with hunger, he had no fight in him. "I'm sorry—truly," he muttered. "Today I have neither copper nor silver to give."

"Then *find* it," Dabasir said flatly. "Surely the son of my old friend can scrape together a few coins to repay a kindness?"

"It's bad luck, sir. Misfortune hounds me—that's why I can't."

"Bad luck?" Dabasir snorted. "Don't blame the gods for your own weakness. *Every* man who borrows but never repays is dogged by 'ill fortune.' Come, boy. I'm hungry, and while I eat, I'll tell you a story."

Tarkad winced at the blunt words—but at least the invitation got him inside the inn. Dabasir steered him to a corner, and they sat on small reed mats.

Kauskor, the proprietor, approached with a grin. Dabasir greeted him in his usual booming style: "Desert lizard! Bring me a juicy goat leg—plenty of bread and all the vegetables in the pot. I'm starving. And for my young friend, a jug of water—make it cool; the day is hot."

Tarkad's stomach knotted. Water for him, a feast for Dabasir. He had no choice but to sit silently, while the smells tortured him.

Dabasir loved an audience. Waving at familiar faces, he launched into conversation. "A traveler from Urfa tells me of a rich man who owns a sheet of stone so thin you can see through it. He set it in his window to keep out the rain, yet through it the whole world looks yellow and strange. What do you think of that, Tarkad? Could the world appear a different color to a man?"

"I suppose so," Tarkad answered, eyes locked on the glistening goat leg now set before Dabasir.

"Well, I have seen the world in false colors myself," Dabasir said, ripping off a hunk of meat. "And this tale will tell you how I learned to see it true again."

"Dabasir's telling a story," one diner whispered, dragging his mat closer. Others did the same, forming a half-circle. They crunched their food loudly, brushing Tarkad with greasy bones, yet no one offered him so much as a crumb.

Dabasir wiped his fingers and began. "Few here know that I was once a slave in Syria."

A ripple of surprise swept the room. Dabasir smiled, pleased.

"When I was young," he continued, "I learned my father's trade—making saddles. I married a good woman, but my skill was still meager, and my income small. I longed for fine things I couldn't afford. Soon merchants trusted me to pay later, so I indulged myself—nice clothes, small luxuries for my wife— always on credit.

"Being young and foolish, I didn't understand that spending more than you earn invites a storm of trouble. As debts piled up, creditors hounded me. I borrowed from friends, couldn't repay, and life turned sour. My wife went back to her father, and I left Babylon, hoping for better luck elsewhere.

"For two restless years I worked for caravans, never finding success. Then I fell in with a band of friendly robbers who preyed on unguarded caravans. Shameful, yes—but I was seeing the world through that 'yellow stone' and didn't notice my own disgrace.

"Our first raid was rich—gold, silks, fine goods—and we squandered it all in Ginir. The second raid failed. A desert chief's spearmen, hired to protect the caravan, struck back. Our leaders died, and the rest of us were hauled to Damascus, stripped naked, and sold as slaves.

"A Syrian chieftain bought me for two silver pieces. My hair was shaved; I wore only a loin cloth. At first I treated it like another adventure—until my master paraded me before his four wives and offered me to them as a eunuch.

"Then I felt true fear. Those desert men were fierce; I had no weapons, no escape.

"I stood trembling while the wives inspected me. Sira, the eldest, stared with a cold, unreadable face—no comfort there. The next was a proud beauty who looked at me as if I were dirt. The two younger ones giggled, thinking it all a grand joke."

It felt like forever as I stood there, waiting for their decision. Each of the four women seemed content to let the others decide my fate. Finally, Sira broke the silence with a cold tone.

"We have enough eunuchs," she said. "But camel tenders—those we lack, and the ones we have are hopeless. Even today I need to visit my sick mother and there's not a single slave I trust to lead my camel. Ask this one if he knows how to tend camels."

My master turned to me. "What do you know about camels?"

Trying to hide my desperation, I answered, "I can make them kneel. I can load them, lead them on long journeys without tiring them. I can even repair their harnesses."

"The slave is bold," my master said. "If you want him, Sira, take him as your camel tender."

So I became hers. That very day, I led her camel on a long journey to her mother's home. On the way, I thanked her for speaking up for me. I told her I wasn't born a slave, but the son of a respected saddle maker from Babylon. I told her my story.

Her response stuck with me.

"How can you call yourself a free man when your weakness brought you here? If a man has the soul of a slave, won't he eventually become one—no matter how he's born? And if a man has the soul of a free man, won't he rise, even after great misfortune?"

I lived as a slave for over a year, but I never became one in spirit. One evening, Sira asked me, "Why do you sit alone in your tent when the others gather together?"

"I'm thinking about what you said," I told her. "I wonder if I really have the soul of a slave. I can't join them. I don't belong with them."

"I sit apart too," she admitted. "My dowry was large—that's why my husband married me. But he doesn't desire me. Every woman wants to be wanted. I can't have children, so I'm pushed aside. If I were a man, I'd rather die than be treated like this. But the rules of our tribe make slaves of women."

"What do you think of me now?" I asked her suddenly. "Do I have the soul of a man—or a slave?"

"Do you want to repay your debts in Babylon?" she asked.

"Yes, but I don't see how."

"If you let the years pass and do nothing, then you have the soul of a slave. A man who doesn't repay his debts can't respect himself—and a man without self-respect *is* a slave."

"But what can I do? I'm a slave in Syria."

"Then stay a slave, you coward."

"I'm no coward!" I shot back.

"Then prove it."

"How?"

"Does your great king not fight his enemies with every strength he has? Your debts are your enemies. They chased you out of Babylon. You ignored them, and they grew too powerful. If you had faced them like a man, you could have conquered them and earned respect. But you didn't have the soul to fight, so here you are—a slave in Syria."

Her words stung deeply. I rehearsed a dozen replies in my head, but I never got the chance to use them.

Three days later, her maid brought me to Sira again.

"My mother is sick. Saddle the two best camels in the herd. Fill the water skins and load food for a long journey."

I did as I was told—but I wondered why so many supplies were packed. Her mother didn't live far.

The maid rode the second camel, and I led the one carrying Sira. When we arrived at her mother's house just after dark, Sira dismissed the maid and turned to me.

"Dabasir," she said, "do you have the soul of a free man or the soul of a slave?"

"The soul of a free man," I said with conviction.

"Then prove it. My husband is drunk and his guards are passed out. Take these camels and escape. Here is a bag of his clothes—use them as a disguise. I will tell them you ran off with the camels while I visited my mother."

"You have the soul of a queen," I told her. "I wish I could lead you to happiness."

"Happiness?" she said softly. "Not for a runaway wife, not in a foreign land. Go. May the gods protect you. The road is long and empty."

That was all I needed. I thanked her and rode off into the night.

I didn't know this country. I barely had a sense of where Babylon lay. But I headed toward the hills—one camel carrying me, the other following.

All night I traveled. All the next day. I was driven by one thought: the brutal punishment for slaves who steal and try to escape.

By the second afternoon, I entered harsh country—rocky, dry, lifeless. The camels stumbled and slowed. No people. No animals. Just the heat and the silence.

What followed was a journey few men survive. Day after day we pressed on. Food ran out. Water ran out. The sun scorched us. On the ninth day, I fell from the camel's back and knew I wouldn't get up again.

I lay on the ground and slept until dawn.

When I awoke, it was quiet. The air was cool. The camels lay nearby, spent and motionless. The land was broken, thorny, empty. No food. No water. Nothing but death.

Was this the end? My mind was clear. My pain was numbed. My thirst and hunger no longer screamed—they just existed.

And then the question came again: *Do I have the soul of a slave, or of a free man?*

If I had the soul of a slave, I would give up, lie down, and die. But if I had the soul of a free man?

Then I would *rise*, find my way back to Babylon, repay those who trusted me, win back my wife, and bring honor to my family.

Sira had said, "Your debts are your enemies." She was right. Why had I run? Why had I let my wife go back to her father?

Then something shifted. It was like the colored glass had been removed from my eyes. I finally saw the world as it truly was.

Die in the desert? Not me.

With new strength, I vowed: I *will* return to Babylon. I *will* repay every debt. I *will* rebuild my life.

My debts were my enemies—but the men I owed were my friends. They had trusted me.

I stood. Weak, staggering—but alive. Hunger didn't matter. Thirst didn't matter. I was a free man on the road home.

Even my camels seemed to understand. Their eyes lit up. Slowly, painfully, they rose and followed me. We pressed forward. We found water. We reached fertile land. We found the road to Babylon.

Because the soul of a free man doesn't whine, "What can I do?" He looks at life's problems—and *solves* them.

I turned to Tarkad.

"What about you? Is your empty belly making your mind sharp? Are you ready to walk the road to self-respect? Do you see the world clearly now? Do you want to pay your debts and be respected again in Babylon?"

Tears welled up in the boy's eyes. He knelt.

"You've shown me a vision," he whispered. "I *feel* the soul of a free man inside me."

Someone nearby asked, "But what happened when you got back?"

Dabasir smiled. "When the will is strong, the way will appear. I had the will, so I found the way. I visited every man I owed. I begged for patience until I could repay them. Some welcomed me. Others mocked me. But one man helped— Mathon, the gold lender.

"He sent me to Nebatur, a camel trader working for the king. I knew camels—and put that knowledge to use. Over time, I repaid every copper, every silver. And finally, I could walk through Babylon with my head high—an honorable man."

Dabasir turned back to his food and called out:

"Kauskor, you lazy snail! My food's cold. Bring fresh meat— and bring a large plate for my young friend Tarkad, the son of my old friend. He's hungry, and today, he eats with me!"

So ended the tale of Dabasir, the Camel Trader of Babylon.

He found his soul the moment he accepted this truth—a truth known by wise men across time:

"Where the determination is, the way can be found."

The Clay Tablets From Babylon

St. Swithin's College
University of Nottingham
Newark-on-Trent, Nottingham

October 21, 1934

Professor Franklin Caldwell
British Scientific Expedition
Hillah, Mesopotamia

Dear Professor Caldwell,

The five clay tablets from your recent dig in the ruins of Babylon arrived on the same boat as your letter. I've been thoroughly captivated and have spent many enjoyable hours translating the inscriptions. I intended to reply sooner, but I held off until I could finish the translations—which I've included with this letter.

Thanks to your excellent preservation methods and careful packing, the tablets arrived in perfect condition.

I must say, you—and we here in the lab—will be amazed at the story these tablets tell. One expects ancient writings to be full of romance and adventure—something straight out of *The Arabian Nights*, perhaps. Instead, we find the very practical tale of a man named Dabasir trying to get out of debt. It's remarkable how little has changed on this old earth over the past five thousand years.

I must admit, these inscriptions struck a personal chord. As a professor, I'm supposed to be reasonably knowledgeable in a variety of fields. And yet, here comes this ancient fellow, emerging from the dusty ruins of Babylon, offering a debt-repayment plan I've never encountered—and one that includes a way to end up with a bit of extra gold in your pocket.

A refreshing idea, I must say! Mrs. Shrewsbury and I are even thinking about trying his plan ourselves—we could certainly use a bit more financial order in our lives.

Wishing you continued success in your important work, and eager for another chance to be of service, I remain,
Sincerely yours,
Alfred H. Shrewsbury
Department of Archaeology

***

Tablet I
As the moon grows full, I, **Dabasir**— lately returned from slavery in Syria—make this permanent record in clay. I am determined to repay all my just debts and become a respected man of means here in Babylon.

Following the wise advice of my friend **Mathon** the gold-lender, I will stick to a precise plan that, he says, can lead any honorable man out of debt and into self-respect.

This plan has three goals, which are my hopes and desires.

First. The plan provides for my future prosperity.

Therefore **one-tenth of everything I earn will be set aside for me to keep**. Mathon speaks wisely:

"A man who keeps gold and silver in his purse, money he doesn't have to spend, is good to his family and loyal to his king. A man with only a few coppers is indifferent to family and king. A man with nothing in his purse becomes bitter, unkind to his family, and disloyal to his king. So anyone who wants to achieve must keep coins jingling in his purse; then love for family and loyalty to king will stay in his heart."

Second. The plan makes sure I support and clothe my good wife, who has loyally returned from her father's house. Mathon says that caring well for a faithful wife puts self-respect in a man's heart and adds strength to his purpose.

So **seven-tenths of all I earn** will pay for our home, clothes, food, and a little extra for pleasure. But Mathon strictly warns that we must **never spend more than seven-tenths** of what I earn on these things. Here lies the plan's success: we must live on that share alone and buy nothing we can't pay for out of it.

***

Tablet II
Third. The plan requires that I pay my debts from my earnings. Whenever the moon is full, **two-tenths of everything I have earned** will be divided, honestly and fairly, among the people who trusted me. In time, every debt will be paid.

Here I carve the name of each creditor and the exact amount
I owe:

- **Fahru** the cloth-weaver—2 silver, 6 copper
- **Sinjar** the couch-maker—1 silver
- **Ahmar**, friend—3 silver, 1 copper
- **Zankar**, friend—4 silver, 7 copper
- **Askamir**, friend—1 silver, 3 copper
- **Harinsir** the jeweler—6 silver, 2 copper
- **Diarbeker**, my father's friend—4 silver, 1 copper
- **Alkahad** the landlord—14 silver
- **Mathon** the gold-lender—9 silver
- **Birejik** the farmer—1 silver, 7 copper
  (The list breaks off here; the rest has crumbled away.)

***

Tablet III
Altogether I owe these creditors **119 silver pieces and 141
copper pieces.**

Because I saw no way to pay, I foolishly let my wife go back
to her father, fled Babylon, chased easy wealth, found only
disaster, and was sold into slavery.

Now that Mathon has shown me how to pay debts with small
shares of my earnings, I see how foolish I was to run from the
results of my extravagance.

I have visited every creditor and explained that I have no
resources except my ability to earn, and that I will put **two-
tenths of all I earn** toward my debts, evenly and honestly. I
can pay no more—but if they are patient, every obligation will
be paid in full.

- **Ahmar,** whom I once thought my best friend, cursed me and I left humiliated.
- **Birejik** begged me to pay him first because he badly needs help.
- **Alkahad** the landlord threatened trouble unless I settled soon.

The rest accepted my proposal. This makes me even more determined. It is easier to pay honest debts than to run from them. Even if I can't satisfy a few creditors' demands, I will treat all of them impartially.

***

Tablet IV
The moon is full again. I have worked hard with a clear mind, and my good wife supports my plan.

Last month, buying sturdy camels for **Nebatur,** I earned **19 silver pieces**.
- I kept one-tenth for myself.
- Seven-tenths paid for our living.
- Two-tenths I divided among the creditors, as evenly as possible in copper.

I didn't see Ahmar, so I left his share with his wife. Birejik was so pleased he kissed my hand. Only old Alkahad grumbled, saying I must pay faster. I told him if I were well fed and not worried, I could pay faster. The others thanked me.

After one month, my debt is down almost four silver pieces, and I have nearly two silver pieces no one else can claim. My heart is lighter than it has been in a long time.

The moon is full again. I worked hard but bought few camels; I earned only **11 silver pieces**. Still, my wife and I kept the plan, buying no new clothes and eating mostly herbs.

- We saved one-tenth.
- Lived on seven-tenths.
- Paid creditors two-tenths.

Ahmar actually praised my payment, small as it was. So did Birejik. Alkahad raged, but when I offered to take his share back if he didn't want it, he calmed down.

Full moon once more—and great joy! I intercepted a fine herd and bought many sound camels; I earned **42 silver pieces**. My wife and I bought needed sandals and clothes and enjoyed good meat and fowl. We paid over eight silver pieces to creditors. Even Alkahad raised no complaint. Truly this plan leads us out of debt and gives us wealth to keep.

Three moons have passed since I last carved these words. Each time:

- I saved one-tenth of everything.
- We lived on seven-tenths, even when it was hard.
- I paid creditors two-tenths.

Now my purse holds **21 silver pieces** that are mine alone. My head is high among friends. My wife keeps a fine home and dresses well. We are happy. This plan—what value! Has it not made an honorable man of a former slave?

***

Tablet V

Full moon again—and I realize it's been long since I wrote on this clay. Twelve moons have passed. **Today I paid the last of my debts.**

My wife and I celebrate with a great feast because our determination has triumphed.

On my final rounds:

- **Ahmar** begged my forgiveness and said he now treasures my friendship.
- "You were once soft clay anyone could shape; now you are bronze that can hold an edge. If you ever need silver or gold, come to me."Old **Alkahad** surprised me:

Many others show me respect. My wife's eyes shine with pride, and that gives a man confidence.

It is the plan that made my success. It let me clear every debt and keep gold and silver jingling in my purse.

I commend it to anyone who wants to move ahead. If it can lift an ex-slave out of debt and leave him with money in hand, can it not help any man find independence?

And I am not finished: I'm convinced that if I keep following this plan, it will make me truly rich.

**WHERE DETERMINATION EXISTS,
THE WAY CAN BE FOUND.**

***

St. Swithin's College
Nottingham University
Newark-on-Trent
Nottingham

Professor Franklin Caldwell
Care of British Scientific Expedition
Hillah, Mesopotamia

November 7, 1936

Dear Professor,

If, in your continued excavations of the Babylonian ruins, you happen to run into the ghost of an old camel trader named **Dabasir**, do me a favor: tell him his clay tablet writings from long ago have earned the lifelong gratitude of a couple of ordinary college folks here in England.

You might recall I wrote you last year that **Mrs. Shrewsbury and I planned to try his plan**—the one about getting out of debt and still having gold to jingle in your pocket. You probably guessed, even though we tried to keep it discreet, that our financial situation had become quite serious.

For years, we struggled under a mountain of old debts. It was humiliating, and we constantly feared that one of our creditors might stir up a scandal that could cost me my position at the college. We paid what we could—every shilling we could scrape together—but it barely made a dent. Worse still, we had to keep buying things on credit, even though it meant paying more.

It turned into one of those vicious cycles that just keeps getting worse. We couldn't even move to a cheaper place because we owed rent to our landlord. We felt trapped— completely hopeless.

And then came **your old friend**, the camel trader from Babylon, with his simple, ancient plan to do exactly what we had tried and failed to do. He inspired us to take action. We made a full list of every debt and personally delivered it to each of our creditors.

I explained to each of them that under our current situation, there was simply no way we could repay everything. The numbers told the story. Then I laid out our plan: we would set aside **20% of our income each month** and divide it fairly among them. At that rate, we'd pay off everything in just over **two years**. Meanwhile, we'd go strictly to cash—**no more credit**—which would benefit them too.

To my surprise, they were actually very reasonable. Our greengrocer, a sharp old fellow, put it plainly:

"If you pay for what you buy and put something toward what you owe, that's better than what you've done in the past three years."

In time, **every creditor agreed not to pressure us**, as long as we kept up regular payments.

Then came the real challenge: learning to live on **70% of our income**. But we were determined to do it—and to keep that extra **10% to jingle in our pockets**.

It became a bit of a game. We scrutinized every expense, starting with rent—where we negotiated a fair reduction. We questioned our usual brand loyalties and often found better quality at lower prices. And we made it work—more easily, and more happily, than we expected.

The best part was the **relief**. The stress of overdue bills vanished. That alone was worth everything.

Now, about that 10% we were supposed to jingle. Well, we *did* jingle it—for a while. But don't laugh—we eventually found it more satisfying **not to spend it**. There's a quiet kind of joy in watching your savings grow.

We ended up investing it in a long-term plan, and we now contribute monthly. That's been the most rewarding part. It's the first thing deducted from my paycheck. There's real peace in knowing our little nest egg is growing steadily. By the time I retire, we should have a tidy sum to live on comfortably.

And all of it is coming from the **same paycheck** I had before. It's hard to believe, but it's true: our **debts are shrinking**, our **savings are growing**, and we're living **better** than ever.

Who would have thought there could be such a dramatic difference between drifting financially and following a **simple plan**?

By the end of next year, when our debts are gone, we plan to **increase our investment contributions**—maybe even take a little trip.

We've made a firm promise to each other: **we'll never again let our lifestyle exceed 70% of our income.**

So now you understand why we wish we could thank that old camel trader ourselves. His plan saved us from what truly felt like **"hell on earth."**

He understood. He had lived it. That's why he carved his story into clay—to help others learn from the wisdom he paid dearly to gain. And now, **five thousand years later,** his words rise again from Babylon's dust—just as powerful, and just as true.

Warm regards,
Alfred H. Shrewsbury
Department of Archaeology

The Luckiest Man in Babylon

At the head of his caravan rode **Sharru Nada**, the merchant prince of Babylon. He was a man who appreciated the finer things—he wore elegant, richly colored robes, and he rode with ease atop his spirited Arabian stallion. Looking at him, you wouldn't guess his age. Nor would anyone suspect that, beneath his composed exterior, he was deeply troubled.

The journey from **Damascus** was long, and the desert held many hardships—but these didn't bother him. The Arab tribes were known to be fierce and eager to plunder wealthy caravans—but even they didn't concern him. His swift and well-armed guards offered more than enough protection.

What troubled him was the **young man** riding beside him— the youth he had brought from Damascus. His name was **Hadan Gula**, the grandson of Sharru Nada's former business partner, **Arad Gula**, to whom he owed a debt of gratitude that could never truly be repaid. He had hoped to do something worthwhile for this grandson, to give him a fresh start. But the more he thought about it, the harder it seemed—because of the young man himself.

Sharru Nada glanced at the boy's flashy rings and earrings.

"He thinks jewelry is for men," he thought. "Still, he has his grandfather's strong features. But Arad Gula would never have worn such flashy robes. Even so, I invited him to come, hoping I could help him rise above the ruins his father made of the family fortune."

His thoughts were interrupted by Hadan Gula himself.

Flashy Dreams, Hard Truths

"Why do you work so hard?" the youth asked. "Why ride with your caravan on all these long trips? Don't you ever stop to enjoy life?"

Sharru Nada smiled.

"Enjoy life?" he repeated. "What would you do to enjoy life— if you were me?"

Hadan Gula answered quickly.

"If I had your wealth, I'd live like a prince. I'd never ride across the hot desert. I'd spend money as fast as it came into my purse. I'd wear the finest robes, the rarest jewels. Now *that* would be living—a life worth having."

Both men laughed.

Sharru Nada spoke again, half-joking.

"Your grandfather never wore jewels." Then, with a teasing grin, he added, "Would you leave no time for work?"

Hadan Gula shrugged.

"Work is for slaves," he said.

Sharru Nada bit his lip but said nothing. They rode in silence for a time, until the trail brought them to a high ridge. Sharru

Nada stopped his horse and pointed toward the green valley in the distance.

"Look," he said, "there's the valley. If you look closely, you can just make out the walls of **Babylon**. That tower over there is the **Temple of Bel**. If your eyes are sharp, you might even see the smoke from the eternal fire burning at its top."

"So that's Babylon?" Hadan Gula said with wonder. "I've always wanted to see the richest city in the world. Babylon— where my grandfather built his fortune. I wish he were still alive. We wouldn't be struggling so much."

"Why wish for his spirit to linger here past its time?" Sharru Nada replied gently. "You and your father are capable of continuing his good work."

Hadan Gula sighed.

"Sadly, neither of us inherited his gift. My father and I have no idea how to attract gold the way he did."

Sharru Nada didn't answer. He loosened the reins and rode silently down the trail into the valley. Behind them, the caravan followed, kicking up a long plume of red dust.

Later, they reached the **King's Highway** and turned south, passing through farmland irrigated by canals.

As they rode, **three old men plowing a field** caught Sharru Nada's eye. He couldn't help but stare. There was something oddly familiar about them.

"Impossible," he thought. "No one passes a field after forty years and finds the same men still working it."

Yet something deep inside insisted they were the same men. One of them gripped the plow awkwardly. The other two trudged along beside the oxen, weakly striking them with their staves to keep them moving.

Forty years ago he had envied those men! How happily he would have traded places with them then. But what a difference now. With pride, he looked back at his own long caravan: carefully chosen camels and donkeys loaded high with valuable goods from Damascus. And that was only one of his many assets.

Pointing at the plowmen, he said, "They're still plowing the same field they worked forty years ago."

"They look the part," Hadan Gula replied, "but why are you so sure they're the same men?"

"I saw them there," Sharru Nada answered.

Memories rushed through his mind. Why couldn't he bury the past and live in the present? Then, as if in a picture, he saw the smiling face of Arad Gula. The wall between him and the cynical youth beside him melted away.

But how could he help such an entitled young man with his lavish tastes and jeweled hands? Sharru Nada could always offer work to anyone willing, but not to someone who felt he was above it. Still, he owed Arad Gula more than a token

The Luckiest Man in Babylon | **131**

effort; they had never done things halfway. That wasn't who they were.

A plan flashed into his head. There were objections—he had to think of his own family and his own reputation. It would be harsh; it would hurt. Being a man of quick decisions, he pushed the objections aside and chose to act.

"Would you like to hear how your worthy grandfather and I started the partnership that made us so successful?" he asked.

"Why not just tell me how you made all that gold?" the young man retorted. "That's all I need to know."

The Slave Chain Begins

Sharru Nada ignored the jab and went on. "Let's start with those men plowing. I was no older than you are now when I first saw them. Our chain-gang was marching by, and good old **Megiddo** the farmer—he was cuffed to me—grumbled about how poorly they were plowing. 'Look at those lazy fellows,' he said. 'The man holding the plow barely scratches the soil, and the others don't keep the oxen in the furrow. How can they hope for a decent harvest with work like that?'"

"You said Megiddo was chained to you?" Hadan Gula asked, surprised.

"Yes—iron collars on our necks with a heavy chain between us. Next to him was **Zabado**, the sheep thief—I'd known him in Harroun. At the end was a man we called *Pirate* because he never gave his name. We guessed he was a sailor—he had intertwined-serpent tattoos across his chest. The guards marched us in rows of four."

"You were a slave?" Hadan Gula asked, incredulous.

"Didn't your grandfather tell you I was once a slave?"

"He spoke of you often but never hinted at that."

"He was the sort of man you could trust with your deepest secrets. You, too, are someone I can trust—am I right?" Sharru Nada looked him straight in the eye.

"You can count on my silence—but I'm amazed. How did you become a slave?"

Sharru Nada shrugged. "Any man can end up a slave. In my case it was a gaming house and barley beer that did me in. My brother killed a friend in a drunken brawl. To save him from prosecution, our father pledged me to the dead man's widow as compensation. When my father couldn't raise enough silver to free me, she angrily sold me to a slave dealer."

"What a terrible injustice!" Hadan Gula exclaimed. "But tell me—how did you win your freedom?"

"We'll get to that, but not yet. Let's keep to the story. When we passed those plowmen, they jeered at us. One even tipped his ragged hat and bowed low, shouting, 'Welcome to Babylon, guests of the king! He's waiting on the city wall with a banquet—mud bricks and onion soup!' They all burst out laughing.

"Pirate flew into a rage and showered them with curses. I asked him, 'What do they mean, the king awaits us on the walls?'

"'To the city walls you march,' he growled, 'to haul bricks until your backs give out. Maybe they'll beat you to death before that. They won't beat me—I'll kill them first.'

"Then Megiddo spoke up. 'It makes no sense for masters to kill hardworking slaves,' he said. 'Good slaves are valuable and get treated well.'

"'Who wants to work hard?' scoffed Zabado. 'Those plowmen know better. They pretend to work so they don't break their backs.'

"'You'll never get ahead by shirking,' Megiddo argued. 'If you plow a full acre, that's an honest day's work; any master sees that. But if you only plow half, you're cheating. I don't cheat. I like to work, and I like to do good work. Work's the best friend I've ever had—it brought me every good thing I owned: my farm, my cows, my crops—everything.'

"'And where are those things now?' taunted Zabado. 'Watch me—I bet I end up with an easy job, carrying the water bag, while you, who love work, break your back hauling bricks.' He let out his silly laugh.

Godoso's Advice and a Spark of Hope
"That night terror gripped me; I couldn't sleep. I crept close to the guard rope, and when the others drifted off, I flagged down **Godoso**, the guard on first watch—one of those cutthroat desert Arabs who'd slice your neck after stealing your purse."

"Tell me, Godoso," I whispered, "when we get to Babylon, will we be sold to the walls?"

"Why do you want to know?" he asked cautiously.

"Don't you understand?" I pleaded. "I'm young. I want to live. I don't want to be worked or beaten to death building walls. Is there any chance I can get a good master?"

He whispered back, "I tell you something. You're a good fellow—don't cause trouble for Godoso. Most times we go first to the slave market. Listen. When buyers come, tell them you're a good worker, say you want to work hard for a good master. Make them want to buy you. If you don't convince them to buy, next day you carry bricks. Very hard work."

After he walked away, I lay in the warm sand staring up at the stars, thinking about work. What Megiddo had said about work being his best friend stuck with me. Could it be mine too? If it could save me from this fate, I would gladly make it my friend.

When Megiddo woke, I whispered the good news to him. It was our one ray of hope as we marched toward Babylon. Late that afternoon, we neared the city walls and could see long lines of men, like black ants, climbing up and down the steep sloped paths. As we got closer, we were astonished by the thousands working: some digging the moat, others mixing dirt into mud for bricks, but most were carrying heavy baskets of bricks up the steep trails to the masons above.

Overseers shouted and cursed at the stragglers, cracking whips over the backs of anyone who didn't stay in line. Exhausted men staggered and collapsed beneath the weight of their loads. If the whip couldn't make them rise, they were shoved off the path and left to writhe in pain. Soon they'd be dragged down to join the others beside the road, waiting for unmarked graves. Seeing all this filled me with dread. This is what awaited my father's son—if I failed at the slave market.

Godoso had been right. We were taken through the gates to the slave prison, and the next morning, we were marched to the market pens. There, the rest of the men huddled in fear. Only the guards' whips kept them moving so the buyers could inspect us. Megiddo and I eagerly spoke to any man who would listen.

The slave dealer brought soldiers from the King's Guard, who chained up Pirate and beat him savagely when he resisted. As they led him away, I felt pity for him.

Megiddo and I knew we would soon be separated. When no buyers were near, he spoke to me earnestly, trying to drive home how valuable work could be to my future:

"Some men hate work. They treat it like an enemy. But it's better to treat it like a friend—learn to enjoy it. Don't mind that it's hard. Think about the house you're building—who cares if the beams are heavy or it's a long way to carry water for the plaster? Promise me this, boy: if you get a master, work as hard as you can for him. If he doesn't appreciate everything you do, don't worry. Remember—work, done well, always benefits the one who does it. It makes him a better man."

He stopped speaking when a large, burly farmer came to the enclosure and started examining us.

Megiddo asked him about his farm and his crops and soon convinced him that he'd make a valuable worker. After some heated bargaining with the slave dealer, the farmer pulled a fat purse from under his robe, and Megiddo followed his new master out of sight.

A few more men were sold that morning. At noon, Godoso quietly told me that the slave dealer was frustrated and would take all the unsold men to the King's buyer at sundown. I was becoming desperate when a fat, friendly-looking man approached the wall and asked if there was a baker among us.

I stepped forward and said, "Why should a good baker like you go looking for another baker with bad habits? Wouldn't it be easier to teach someone willing—like me—your skilled ways? Look at me—I'm young, strong, and I love to work. Give me a chance, and I'll do my best to earn gold and silver for your purse."

A New Master, A New Beginning

He seemed impressed by my attitude and started bargaining with the dealer, who—until that moment—had barely noticed me. Now he suddenly became eloquent, praising my skills, health, and good nature. I felt like a fat ox being sold at the market. But finally, to my joy, the deal was done. I followed my new master away, thinking I must be the luckiest man in all of Babylon.

My new home pleased me greatly. Nana-naid, my master, taught me how to grind barley in the stone bowl in the courtyard, how to build a fire in the oven, and how to grind the sesame flour for honey cakes. I had a sleeping mat in the shed where the grain was stored. The old housekeeper, Swasti, fed me well and liked how I helped her with the heavy chores.

This was the opportunity I had longed for—to prove my value to my master, and maybe, one day, to earn my freedom.

I asked Nana-naid to teach me how to knead the bread and bake it. He was happy to do so, pleased with my eagerness. Later, when I could bake bread well, I asked him to teach me how to make honey cakes. Soon I was doing all the baking myself. My master was glad to relax, though Swasti disapproved.

"Having no work is bad for any man," she warned.

I knew it was time to think of a way to start earning money to buy my freedom. Since the baking was finished by noon, I figured Nana-naid might let me use my afternoons for profit—and maybe even share in the earnings. Then I had an idea: why not bake extra honey cakes and sell them on the streets of the city?

I presented my plan like this: "If I use my afternoons, after baking, to earn coins for you, wouldn't it be fair for you to share some of those coins with me—so I could have money of my own to spend on things every man wants and needs?"

"Fair enough, fair enough," he agreed.

When I told him my plan to peddle the honey cakes, he was pleased. "Here's what we'll do," he said. "You sell them at two for a penny. Half of the pennies go to me to cover the flour, honey, and firewood. From what's left, I'll take half and you'll keep half."

I was thrilled with his generous offer—to keep one-fourth of all sales for myself. That night, I worked late making a tray to display the cakes. Nana-naid gave me one of his old robes so I'd look presentable, and Swasti helped me patch and clean it.

Work Pays Its First Dividends

The next day I baked an extra batch of honey-cakes. They looked perfectly browned and tempting on my tray as I walked the streets, calling out my wares. At first no one seemed interested and I grew discouraged, but I kept at it. Later in the afternoon, when people began to feel hungry, the cakes started to sell, and soon my tray was empty.

Nana-naid was delighted with my success and gladly paid me my share. I was thrilled to have real money of my own. Megiddo had been right—masters do value good work from their slaves. That night I was so excited I could barely sleep; I tried to calculate how much I could earn in a year, and how many years it would take to buy my freedom.

The Rug Merchant and the Slave

Out selling every day, I soon found regular customers. One of them was your grandfather, Arad Gula. He was a rug merchant who made house-to-house calls all over the city, with a donkey piled high with rugs and a black slave to lead it. He would buy two cakes for himself and two for his slave, always pausing to chat with me while they ate.

One day your grandfather said something I've never forgotten: "I like your cakes, boy, but I like even more the spirit with which you sell them. That kind of energy can carry you far."

You can't imagine what encouraging words like that meant to a lonely slave boy in a big city, fighting as hard as he could to escape humiliation.

As the months passed, the pennies in my purse began to add up, and the weight of it on my belt felt wonderfully comforting. Work was proving to be my best friend, just as Megiddo had said. I was happy—but Swasti was worried.

"Your master spends too much time in the gambling houses," she fretted. "He's losing heavily; I fear for him."

I was overjoyed to run into Megiddo one day, leading three donkeys loaded with vegetables to market. "I'm doing well," he beamed. "My master values my work—now I'm a foreman. See? He trusts me to handle the marketing, and he's even sending for my family. Work is helping me recover from my great trouble. Someday it will buy my freedom, and I'll own a farm again."

Time went on, and Nana-naid grew more anxious for me to come back quickly from selling. He'd be waiting to count and divide the money, and he urged me to find more buyers and increase sales.

I often went outside the city gates to the overseers of the slaves building the walls. I hated seeing those grim sights again, but the overseers were good customers. One day I was shocked to spot Zabado waiting in line to fill a brick basket. He was gaunt and bent, his back covered with welts and sores from the whip. I felt sorry for him and handed him a cake, which he crammed into his mouth like a starving animal.

Seeing the greed in his eyes, I ran before he could grab my tray.

"Why do you work so hard?" Arad Gula asked me one day—almost the same question you asked earlier, remember? I told him what Megiddo had said about work and showed him my purse of pennies, explaining how I was saving to buy my freedom.

"What will you do once you're free?" he asked.

"I intend to become a merchant," I said.

Then he confided something I had never suspected. "You don't know I'm a slave too. I'm in partnership with my master."

"Stop!" Hadan Gula burst out. "I won't listen to lies that smear my grandfather. He wasn't a slave." His eyes flashed with anger.

Sharru Nada stayed calm. "I honor him for rising above misfortune and becoming a leading citizen of Damascus. Are you, his grandson, made of the same metal? Can you face facts, or would you rather live under illusions?"

Hadan Gula straightened in the saddle. In a voice tight with emotion he said, "My grandfather was loved by everyone. When famine came, didn't his gold buy grain in Egypt, and didn't his caravan bring it to Damascus so no one starved? And now you say he was a despised slave in Babylon?"

"If he had remained a slave in Babylon, perhaps. But through his own efforts he became a great man in Damascus. The gods honored him," Sharru Nada replied.

He went on: "After he told me he was a slave, he confessed how eager he was to buy his freedom. But business had slowed, and he feared leaving his master's protection. I scolded him: 'Stop clinging to your master. Act like a free man if you want to be one. Decide what you want and let work help you get it.' He left, glad I'd shamed his cowardice.

"Soon after, I went beyond the gates again and found a huge crowd gathering. A man told me, 'Haven't you heard? A runaway slave who killed one of the King's guards will be flogged to death today. Even the King is coming.'

"The crowd was so thick I climbed the unfinished wall to see over their heads. I saw Nebuchadnezzar himself ride by in his golden chariot—such splendor! I couldn't see the flogging itself, but I heard the screams. I wondered how a noble king could laugh and joke while such cruelty went on—but then I understood why the wall-slaves were driven so mercilessly.

"When the slave was dead, they hung his body upside down so all could see. After the crowd scattered, I went closer—and on his chest I saw tattooed two entwined serpents. It was Pirate.

"The next time I met Arad Gula, he was a changed man, full of energy. 'Look,' he said, 'the slave you knew is now free! Your words were magic. My sales and profits are climbing, and my wife is overjoyed. She was born free—the niece of my master. She wants us to move to another city where no one knows I was ever a slave, so our children won't bear that stigma. Work has become my best helper; it's brought back my confidence.'

"I was thrilled that I'd repaid him, even a little, for the encouragement he gave me.

Freedom Bought at a Price

"One evening Swasti came to me in distress. 'Your master is in trouble,' she said. 'Months ago he lost heavily at the gaming tables. He hasn't paid the farmer for grain or the moneylender for his loan. They're furious and threaten him.'

"'Why should we worry?' I said foolishly. 'We're not his keepers.'

"'You don't understand,' she cried. 'To the moneylender he pledged your title for collateral. He can claim you and sell you.' Her fears were real. The next morning, while I was baking, the moneylender returned with a man named Sasi. They said the debt was due and took me on the spot. All I had was the robe on my back and my purse of pennies, which I hid under the robe.

"Sasi was rough and curt. As he dragged me across the city, I told him of my good work for Nana-naid and promised to work just as hard for him. He only grunted. 'My master hates this job,' he said. 'The King ordered him to send me to build a section of the Grand Canal. He told me to buy more slaves, work them hard, finish quick. Bah! How can any man finish a big job quick?'

The Brutal Canal Fields

"Picture a desert with no trees, just low shrubs and a sun so fierce the water in our skins grew too hot to drink. Picture endless lines of men hauling heavy baskets of dirt from dawn till dark. We slept on the bare ground and ate from troughs, like pigs. That's where I landed. I buried my purse of pennies under a marked spot, wondering if I'd ever dig it up again."

At first, I worked willingly. But as the months dragged on, I felt my spirit breaking. Then the fever from the brutal heat took hold of my worn-out body. I lost my appetite and could barely eat the mutton and vegetables. At night I tossed and turned, unable to sleep.

In my misery, I started to wonder if Zabado had the right idea—to slack off and save his back from breaking under the weight of labor. But then I remembered the last time I saw him, and I knew his plan had failed.

I thought about Pirate and his bitterness. Maybe fighting back and killing was the way—but the memory of his bloody, lifeless body reminded me that his path was useless, too.

Then I recalled my last glimpse of Megiddo. His hands were thick with callouses from hard work, but his heart was light, and his face shone with joy. He had chosen the best way.

Despair and Reflection

I was just as willing to work as Megiddo—surely I couldn't have worked any harder than I did. So why didn't my work bring me the same joy and success? Was it really work that gave Megiddo happiness, or were happiness and success just gifts from the gods? Was I doomed to spend my whole life working without ever reaching my dreams—without joy or reward?

All these questions swirled in my head. I had no answers. I was completely confused.

A few days later, when I thought I had reached my limit and still didn't know what to do, Sasi summoned me. A messenger had arrived from my old master, ordering my return to Babylon. I dug up my precious little wallet, wrapped myself in the torn remains of my robe, and began the journey back.

As we rode, those same thoughts of being tossed around like a leaf in a storm kept spinning through my feverish mind. I felt like I was living the strange old chant from my hometown of Harroun:

Whirled by winds like a storm,
Driven with no control,
A path no man can follow,
A future no one can know.

Was I always going to suffer like this—for reasons I didn't even understand? What new hardships and disappointments lay ahead?

A Brother Returns

When we arrived at my master's courtyard, imagine my shock to see Arad Gula waiting for me. He helped me down and embraced me like a long-lost brother.

As we walked, I followed him like a slave would follow his master. But he wouldn't allow it. He threw his arm around me and said, "I searched everywhere for you. I had nearly lost hope when I found Swasti. She told me about the moneylender, who led me to your new master. It took a hard bargain—he made me pay a ridiculous price—but you were worth every coin. Your mindset and drive inspired me to change my life."

"Megiddo's mindset, not mine," I corrected.

"Megiddo's and yours," he said. "Thanks to both of you, we're going to Damascus. And I need you as my partner. Look!" he exclaimed. "In one moment, you'll be a free man!"

He pulled a clay tablet from under his robe—my title of ownership. Holding it high above his head, he smashed it on the cobblestones. Then he stomped on the shards until they were nothing but dust.

Tears filled my eyes. I knew I was the luckiest man in Babylon.

You see—work had proven to be my best friend, even in my darkest hour. Because I was willing to work, I avoided being sold to those miserable wall-building gangs. And it was my work ethic that impressed your grandfather so deeply he chose me as his partner.

The Truth About Your Grandfather

Then Hadan Gula asked, "Was work the secret to my grandfather's golden wealth?"

"It was the only key he had when I first met him," Sharru Nada replied. "Your grandfather loved to work. The gods respected his efforts and rewarded him richly."

"I think I'm beginning to understand," Hadan Gula said thoughtfully. "Work attracted friends who admired his diligence and the success it brought him. Work earned him the honors he enjoyed in Damascus. Work gave him everything I respect—and I used to think work was only for slaves."

"Life has many pleasures for men to enjoy," Sharru Nada said. "Each has its place. I'm just glad work isn't reserved only for slaves. If it were, I'd miss out on my greatest joy. I enjoy many things—but nothing replaces the satisfaction of work."

As Sharru Nada and Hadan Gula rode under the looming shadows of Babylon's massive bronze gates, the guards snapped to attention and saluted the respected citizen. With his head held high, Sharru Nada led his long caravan through the gates and up the city's streets.

A Change of Heart

"I've always wanted to be like my grandfather," Hadan Gula admitted. "But until today, I didn't really understand what kind of man he was. Now that I know, I admire him even more—and I'm determined to follow his example. I doubt I can ever repay you for revealing the real key to his success. From this day on, I will use it. I'll begin humbly, just like he did—which suits me far better than flashy jewelry and fancy clothes."

So saying, Hadan Gula took off the jeweled earrings and rings from his fingers. Then he pulled back on the reins and respectfully rode behind the leader of the caravan.

An Historical Sketch of Babylon

No city in history has sounded more glamorous than Babylon. Just hearing the name calls up images of dazzling wealth— gold, jewels, and endless splendor. You might picture such riches tucked into a lush tropical setting, surrounded by forests and mines. In truth, Babylon had none of that.

It sat beside the Euphrates River, smack-dab in a flat, bone-dry valley. There were no forests to log, no stone to quarry, and no metal ores to mine. It wasn't even on a major trade route. Rainfall was so skimpy that farmers couldn't rely on it for crops.

So where did the wealth come from? From people. Babylon is history's showcase of what human creativity and grit can accomplish with limited raw materials. Every resource that fed the city was developed by human hands; every ounce of its wealth was man-made.

Babylon's *only* natural advantages were fertile soil and a steady river. The rest was pure engineering. Early Babylonian builders threw dams across the Euphrates and dug gigantic irrigation canals, some running miles into the desert. Water that once rushed past unused now fanned out over dry ground and turned it into super-productive farmland. Historians rank those canals among humankind's first great engineering marvels—and the lush harvests that followed had no equal in the ancient world.

Through most of its long life, Babylon was steered by pragmatic rulers. They fought when necessary, but conquest and looting weren't their main goals. Instead, their reputations rest on wise policies, ambitious projects, and fair laws. Babylon never produced a glory-hungry emperor bent on world domination; it prospered through brains, not bragging.

Time eventually drained away the energy that kept Babylon humming. Without constant upkeep the city crumbled and, within a few generations, became a desolate ruin.

Where Babylon Stood

Babylon's ruins lie in modern-day Iraq, roughly 600 miles east of the Suez Canal and just north of the Persian Gulf—about the same latitude as Yuma, Arizona. The climate is likewise hot and dry. Today the once-fertile Euphrates Valley is mostly empty desert scrub, grazed by a few nomadic herders.

For centuries, travelers mistook the low earthen mounds dotting the plain for ordinary hills. Only when storms exposed fragments of brick and pottery did archaeologists investigate. European and American teams soon proved the "hills" were buried cities—Babylon among them. Two thousand years of wind and weather had reduced its brick walls to dust and rubble, but by digging through the layers, researchers have reopened its streets, temples, and palaces.

Many scholars consider Babylonian culture—along with that of neighboring Sumer—the world's oldest well-documented civilization, with securely dated records stretching back 8,000 years. How do we know the dates? One clay tablet described a solar eclipse. Modern astronomers calculated exactly when that eclipse would have been visible in Babylon, connecting their calendar to ours.

By 6,000 B.C. the Sumerians already lived in walled cities. They weren't primitive cave dwellers either: they were the first known engineers, astronomers, mathematicians, financiers, and the first people who wrote things down.

Engineering Feats

We've mentioned the vast irrigation network that turned desert into farmland. Remains of those canals are still visible—some so wide that, when empty, a dozen horses could gallop side by side along the bottom. The Babylonians also drained a massive marsh at the mouth of the Euphrates and Tigris Rivers, converting it into fertile fields.

The Greek historian Herodotus toured Babylon at its height and wrote vivid notes. He marveled at the soil's incredible yield of wheat and barley—direct results of that irrigation.

Written on Clay

Babylon's wisdom survives because its people didn't use perishable paper. They pressed letters into wet clay tablets about six by eight inches and an inch thick, then baked them rock hard. They recorded myths, poems, laws, contracts, property deeds, promissory notes—even personal letters couriered to other towns. Whole libraries—hundreds of thousands of tablets—have been unearthed, giving us a front-row seat to their daily lives.

The Mighty Walls

Ancient writers ranked Babylon's city walls among the Seven Wonders of the World, rivaled only by Egypt's Great Pyramid. Queen Semiramis supposedly built the first set, though no trace of those remains. Later walls, begun around 600 B.C. by King Nabopolassar and finished by his son

Nebuchadnezzar, were truly colossal: roughly 160 feet high, up to eleven miles long, and thick enough for a six-horse chariot to race along the top. Outside was a deep water-filled moat. Today only the foundations and parts of the moat survive—later generations quarried the brick for their own buildings.

Siege-Proof City

Wave after wave of ancient armies laid siege to Babylon but never broke through the walls. These were no small forces: chronicles speak of 10,000 cavalry, 25,000 chariots, and infantry by the thousands. Commanders spent years stockpiling supplies before marching. Yet Babylon held out—until 539 B.C., when Cyrus of Persia captured the city without breaching the walls. The Babylonian king met him in open battle, lost, and retreated; Cyrus simply walked through the undefended gates.

After that, Babylon's influence faded. Within a few centuries it was abandoned entirely, left to wind and sand.

What Babylon Gave the World

Even in ruins, Babylon shaped civilization. Its people pioneered:

- **Mathematics and astronomy**
- **Metal tools and weapons** while other societies still used stone
- **Artistic sculpture, textiles, and fine jewelry**
- **Contracts, promissory notes, and the very concept of money** as a standard medium of exchange

Their economic savvy let merchants, farmers, and craftsmen thrive. The clay-tablet records show complex loans, deeds, and business partnerships that feel strikingly modern.

A Lasting Lesson

Babylon's monuments are dust, but its knowledge endures. Six thousand years ago, prosperous Babylonians learned— and wrote down—the same simple laws of money that still govern wealth today:

- **Money measures earthly success.**
- **Money lets us enjoy life's best offerings.**
- **Money is abundant for anyone who understands the rules for getting it.**
- **Those rules have never changed—whether on Babylon's brick streets or in the financial centers of the modern world.**

The story of Babylon proves that determined people, using brains and sweat instead of natural advantages, can build unimaginable wealth—and that the principles behind that wealth never go out of date.

www.ingramcontent.com/pod-product-compliance
Lightning Source LLC
Chambersburg PA
CBHW031857200326
41597CB00012B/457